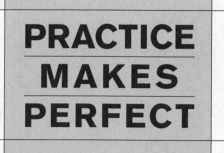

PRACTICE
MAKES
PERFECT

German
Sentence Builder

Ed Swick

McGraw Hill

New York   Chicago   San Francisco   Lisbon   London   Madrid   Mexico City
Milan   New Delhi   San Juan   Seoul   Singapore   Sydney   Toronto

P9-DID-138

The **McGraw-Hill** Companies

Copyright © 2009 by The McGraw-Hill Companies, Inc. All rights reserved. Printed in
the United States of America. Except as permitted under the United States Copyright
Act of 1976, no part of this publication may be reproduced or distributed in any form
or by any means, or stored in a database or retrieval system, without the prior written
permission of the publisher.

9 10 11 12 13 14 15 16 17   QVS/QVS   1 9 8 7 6 5

ISBN   978-0-07-159962-7
MHID   0-07-159962-2

Library of Congress Control Number: 2008939101

Trademarks: McGraw-Hill, the McGraw-Hill Publishing logo, Practice Makes Perfect,
and related trade dress are trademarks or registered trademarks of The McGraw-Hill
Companies and/or its affiliates in the United States and other countries and may not
be used without written permission. All other trademarks are the property of their
respective owners. The McGraw-Hill Companies is not associated with any product or
vendor mentioned in this book.

McGraw-Hill books are available at special quantity discounts to use as premiums
and sales promotions, or for use in corporate training programs. To contact a
representative, please e-mail us at bulksales@mcgraw-hill.com.

This book is printed on acid-free paper.

To Riane, AJ, Jalyn, Tori, and Riley, my terrific grandkids.

Contents

Acknowledgments

I wish to extend my gratitude to Stefan Feyen for all his help and suggestions.

Introduction

Writing skills are usually the most difficult skills to acquire in a language. This is particularly true in a foreign language. The goal of this book is to guide you through the various types of structures in the German language and to illustrate how those structures combine to make sentences.

Naturally, in order to acquire writing skills you have *to write*. Therefore, you will be provided with an abundance of writing exercises. Some will require a small variation in a given sentence. Others will provide you with a series of words that you form into an appropriate sentence. And you will have plenty of opportunity for coming up with original sentences of your own. This development of your German sentence writing moves gradually and with careful explanation from the least complex activity to the most complex.

Make changes to given sentences.
Combine a series of words as a sentence. ⎫ Writing skills developed
Write original sentences. ⎭

In addition to the illustrations of how structures combine to form sentences, and the practice exercises, an answer key is provided at the end of the book. It includes not only the correct answers for the exercises but also sample sentences for you to use to compare to your original sentences.

Good sentence writing is not an impossible task. But it requires analysis and practice and a willingness to apply concepts and rules consistently. Let this book guide you, and you will discover a new confidence as you write more successfully in German.

Viel Glück!

Declarative sentences and word order

Declarative sentences in both English and German consist of a subject and a predicate. In German, the subject is in the nominative case, and the verb in the predicate is conjugated appropriately for the subject and in a specific tense:

> **subject + verb + predicate**
> Karl + singt + gut.
> *Karl sings well.*

In the example sentence above, the subject is **Karl** and the verb **singt** is conjugated in the present tense for the third person singular subject. This basic structure is used in great abundance in the language and can be modified in a variety of ways. Nonetheless, its simple formula is *subject plus predicate*. If one of those elements is missing, you don't have a sentence.

Let's look at a series of sentences composed in this way. Take note of the subjects, the variety of verb types in the predicate, and the various tenses that can be used in declarative sentences. Many sentences are composed of a present perfect tense verb and the auxiliary **haben**:

> Karin hat in Leipzig gewohnt.   *Karin lived in Leipzig.*

Many are composed of a present perfect tense verb and the auxiliary **sein**:

> Sie sind nach Kanada   *They emigrated to Canada.*
> ausgewandert.

Many appear in the future tense with the auxiliary **werden**:

> Die Kinder werden im Garten   *The children will play in the garden.*
> spielen.

Others can be a combination of a modal auxiliary and an infinitive:

> Niemand kann ihn verstehen.   *No one can understand him.*

And still others can be written in the passive voice:

> Deutsch wird hier gesprochen.   *German is spoken here.*

In other words, a declarative sentence can take many forms.

Rewrite the following declarative sentences in the missing tenses.

1. Present   Martin spricht kein Englisch.

   Past   a. _____

   Present perfect   b. _____

   Future   c. _____

2. Present   a. _____

   Past   b. _____

   Present perfect   c. _____

   Future   Ich werde es machen können.

3. Present   a. _____

   Past   b. _____

   Present perfect   Eine Schlange hat den Frosch gefressen.

   Future   c. _____

4. Present   a. _____

   Past   Über dem Wald flogen viele Vögel.

   Present perfect   b. _____

   Future   c. _____

Negation

Declarative sentences do not always make positive statements. They can be made negative by adding a negative word to the sentence or by changing a positive subject to a negative subject.

The most common way to negate a sentence is by the addition of the adverb **nicht** (*not*):

Karl singt gut.   *Karl sings well.*
Karl singt nicht gut.   *Karl doesn't sing well.*

German usually places **nicht** in front of the element that is negated. However, if that element is the verb itself, **nicht** follows the conjugated form or stands between the auxiliary and the corresponding infinitive or participle. **Nicht** also follows an adverb or adverbial phrase that describes *time* or *place* or an object that is in the *accusative case*:

Es geht nicht.   *That won't work.*
Sie sind nicht zu Hause gewesen.   *They weren't at home.*
Er konnte gestern nacht nicht schlafen.   *He couldn't sleep last night.*
Sie kennt den Mann nicht.   *She doesn't know the man.*

Nicht precedes a prepositional phrase or an adverbial that describes the *manner* in which something was done:

> **subject + verb + nicht + prepositional phrase**
> Sie + fahren + nicht + nach Hause.
> *They're not driving home.*

English often requires the auxiliary *do/does* when negating. This does not occur in German:

Sie warten nicht auf Katrin.	*They **don't** wait for Katrin.*
Er versteht nicht.	*He **doesn't** understand.*
Onkel Fritz kommt nicht heute.	*Uncle Fritz isn't coming today.*

When negating a noun, **kein** (*no, not any*) is used:

> **kein + noun**
> keine + Bücher
> *no/not any books*

Ich habe kein Geld.	*I don't have any money.*
Jack kennt keine Deutschen.	*Jack doesn't know any Germans.*
Es dauert keine fünf Minuten.	*It won't last more than five minutes.*

Übung

1·2

*Rewrite each sentence, negating the underlined element with **nicht**.*

EXAMPLE: Sie laufen in den Garten.

Sie laufen nicht in den Garten.

1. Das ist das beste Buch.

   _____

2. Sie ist am Nachmittag angekommen.

   _____

3. Ihr Mann ist bei einem Unglück umgekommen.

   _____

4. Er hat helfen wollen.

   _____

5. Frau Schneider hat sich wohl gefühlt.

   _____

6. Die Studenten sitzen im Lesesaal.

   _____

7. Seine Frau hat ihn betrogen.

   _____

*Rewrite each sentence, negating the underlined element with **kein**.*

EXAMPLE: Luise hat die Zeitung.

Luise hat keine Zeitung.

1. Meine Großmutter trinkt Kaffee.

_____

2. Boris hat interessante Bücher gefunden.

_____

3. Die Jungen haben den Kindern geholfen.

_____

4. Der Dieb hat ein Wort gesagt.

_____

5. In diesem Wald gibt es Bären.

_____

6. Ich werde das unter diesen Umständen tun.

_____

*Rewrite each sentence, negating the underlined element with **kein** or **nicht**, whichever is appropriate.*

1. Ihr Sohn hat mitgehen wollen.

_____

2. Die Leute gehen in seinen Laden.

_____

3. Ich klebte die Marke auf den Brief.

_____

4. Der Bodensee ist der größte See.

_____

5. Ein Mann spricht mit ihm.

_____

6. Die Lehrerin brauchte <u>einen Kugelschreiber</u>.

_____

7. Der betrunkene Mann fährt <u>schnell</u>.

_____

Niemand, nichts, and niemals

The negative pronouns **niemand** (*no one, nobody*) and **nichts** (*nothing*) are high-frequency words and are commonly used to negate a sentence. The same is true of the adverb **nie** or **niemals** (*never*). **Niemand** and **nichts** can act as subjects or objects. Compare their use in the following examples:

Niemand besucht sie.	*No one is visiting them.*
Sie versteht niemanden.	*She doesn't understand anybody.*
Nichts interessiert ihn.	*Nothing interests him.*
Ich habe nichts für die Kinder.	*I have nothing for the children.*

Nie / niemals is used adverbially:

Er geht nie (niemals) ins Kino.	*He never goes to the movies.*

Just like **jemand**, **niemand** can have a declensional ending in the accusative and dative cases. That ending, however, is optional:

Nominative	jemand	niemand
Accusative	jemand *or* jemanden	niemand *or* niemanden
Dative	jemand *or* jemandem	niemand *or* niemandem

Übung
1·5

Change the underlined word(s) in each sentence to the appropriate negative word: ***niemand, nichts,*** *or* ***nie (niemals)***.

EXAMPLE: Thomas hat <u>zehn Euro</u>.

Thomas hat nichts.

1. <u>Die Mädchen</u> wollen Schlittschuh laufen.

_____

2. Der Polizist wird <u>den Dieb</u> verhaften.

_____

3. Manfred geht <u>alle paar Tage</u> in die Stadt.

_____

4. Meine Verwandten waren <u>gestern</u> in Berlin.

_____

5. Sonja wird <u>ihre kranke Tante</u> in Hamburg besuchen.

_____

6. Er will <u>etwas</u> zu essen haben.

_____

Word order

The sentences you have encountered so far all began with the subject of the sentence. But German sentences can begin with other elements as well. When this occurs, the verb in the sentence will precede the subject. Consider the following sentences. Notice that the English sentences cannot always follow the German word order, particularly when the German sentence begins with a direct object:

ADVERB	**Gestern** war er in der Stadt.	_Yesterday he was in the city._
DIRECT OBJECT	**Das** verstehe ich nicht.	_I don't understand that._
CLAUSE	**Als ich in Berlin war**, besuchte ich meinen Onkel.	_When I was in Berlin, I visited my uncle._

In the previous examples, the various German sentences began with an adverb (**Gestern**), a direct object (**Das**), and a clause (**Als ich in Berlin war**). And in each case the subject was preceded by the verb:

non-subject element + verb + subject → inverted subject and verb

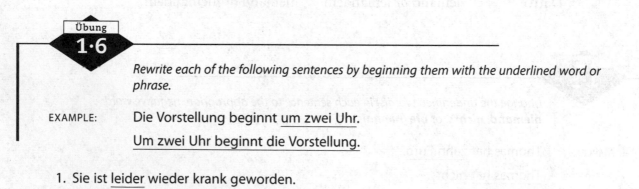

Übung
1·6

Rewrite each of the following sentences by beginning them with the underlined word or phrase.

EXAMPLE: Die Vorstellung beginnt <u>um zwei Uhr</u>.

<u>Um zwei Uhr beginnt die Vorstellung.</u>

1. Sie ist <u>leider</u> wieder krank geworden.

_____

2. Martin blieb <u>den ganzen Tag</u> zu Hause.

_____

3. Ich verbringe <u>meine Freizeit</u> in der Bibliothek.

_____

4. Ich begegnete meinen Nachbarn, <u>als ich um die Ecke kam</u>.

_____

5. Ich möchte <u>im Herbst</u> nach Italien reisen.

_____

6. Sie geht oft ins Theater, <u>wenn sie in London ist</u>.

_____

It is important to remember that German sentences that begin with some element other than the subject cannot always be translated word for word into English. For example:

Den Mann beißt der Hund.

Those words translate as _the man bites the dog_, but the German sentence begins with the direct object and must, therefore, be translated into English as _the dog bites the man_.

Übung

1·7

Rewrite each of the following sentences by placing the direct object at the beginning of the sentence.

EXAMPLE: Der Hund beißt den Mann.
            <u>Den Mann beißt der Hund.</u>

1. Er hat den Wecker reparieren lassen.

_____

2. Sie wissen das nicht.

_____

3. Die Jungen spielen Schach.

_____

4. Man muss das nicht.

_____

5. Die Frau kaufte einen Mantel im Kaufhaus.

_____

Rewrite the following sentences by beginning each one first with an adverb, then with a prepositional phrase, and finally with a clause of your choosing.

1. Meine Familie isst italienisch.

   a. Adverb _____

   b. Prepositional phrase _____

   c. Clause _____

2. Sonja spielte Tennis.

   a. Adverb _____

   b. Prepositional phrase _____

   c. Clause _____

3. Seine Freundin wird einen neuen Wagen kaufen.

   a. Adverb _____

   b. Prepositional phrase _____

   c. Clause _____

Compose sentences using the words provided in each list. Add any necessary words.

EXAMPLE: morgen / kommen / er / mit / Freund / nach Hause

Morgen kommt er mit einem Freund nach Hause.

1. in / Woche / werden / wir / wieder / Wien / sein

   _____

2. Mutter / müssen / um / sechs / aufstehen / und / Stadt / fahren

   _____

3. als / ich / in / Hauptstadt / sein / gehen / ich / oft / Museum

   _____

Write original sentences. Begin each one with the cue words provided.

EXAMPLE: (heute)

Heute werde ich meine Tante in Berlin besuchen.

1. (jemand)

   _____

2. (vor einer Woche)

   _____

3. (um zehn Uhr)

   _____

Interrogative sentences

In both English and German, there is a variety of ways to form questions. In German questions that concern the action of a verb and in some English questions, the verb precedes the subject:

> **verb + subject**
> Ist + Martin zu Hause?
> *Is Martin at home?*

But if the question concerns the action of a verb, English most often uses the auxiliary *to do* to form the question. For example:

> **verb + subject**
> Sprechen + Sie Deutsch?
> *Do you speak German?*

> **verb + subject**
> Kaufte + er einen Mantel?
> *Did he buy a coat?*

With the verb *to be* and sometimes with the verb *to have*, however, the auxiliary *to do* is not needed in English. Instead, as in German, the question begins with the verb:

Ist sie wieder krank?	*Is she sick again?*
Waren sie in München?	*Were they in Munich?*
Haben Sie keinen Pass?	*Have you no passport?*

If the verb *to have* is transitive, a question can be formed either with the auxiliary verb *to do* or without it. However, the form that uses *to do* is more common in modern English:

Hast du genug Geld?	*Do you have enough money?* or *Have you enough money?*
Hatten sie kein Handy?	*Didn't they have a cell phone?* or *Had they no cell phone?*

If the verb *to have* is the auxiliary of a perfect tense, the auxiliary verb *to do* cannot be used in the formation of a question:

Hat er sein Heft gefunden?	*Has he found his notebook?*
Hatte Sonja ihre Tasche verloren?	*Had Sonja lost her purse?*

The auxiliary *to do* is used in English questions only in the present and past tenses with the exception, of course, of *to be* and *to have* as illustrated in the previous examples. The English future tense also avoids using *to do* in a question. Other auxiliaries, such as certain modal auxiliaries, also avoid it:

Wirst du auch mitkommen?	*Will you come along, too?*
Kannst du mir helfen?	*Can you help me?*

If the English modal requires the particle word *to* in order to complete its meaning, use *to do* to form a question. *To be able to* is an exception to this rule, because the verb *to be* is involved:

to be able to	*Are you able to breathe all right?*
to have to	*Does he have to shout like that?*
to need to	*Did the dogs need to be fed?*

The point being made here is that it is important to realize that you cannot translate English questions directly into German. You have to look at the structure of the English sentence and modify for the German approach to forming questions for the action of a verb: *the verb precedes the subject in a German question:*

verb + subject → eine Frage

Let's look at a few examples:

Statement: Er singt sehr gut.	*He sings very well.*
Question: Singt er sehr gut?	*Does he sing very well?*
Statement: Sie ging nach Hause.	*She went home.*
Question: Ging sie nach Hause?	*Did she go home?*

The same word order is required when a modal is used in the sentence:

Statement: Du musst so oft rauchen.	*You have to smoke so often.*
Question: Musst du so oft rauchen?	*Do you have to smoke so often?*

If the sentence is in the present perfect tense, the auxiliary verb precedes the subject.

Statement: Der Mann ist gestorben.	*The man has died.*
Question: Ist der Mann gestorben?	*Has the man died?*

In a future tense sentence, the auxiliary **werden** precedes the subject:

Statement: Wir werden mit ihm reisen.	*We will travel with him.*
Question: Werden wir mit ihm reisen?	*Will we travel with him?*

Übung
2·1

Rewrite each statement as a question.

1. Sein Vetter ist in der Hauptstadt gewesen.

   _____

2. Gudrun will die Wahrheit über das Unglück erfahren.

   _____

3. Die kranke Frau litt an einer Vergiftung.

   _____

4. Man muss alle Verkehrszeichen beachten.

_____

5. Ich durfte Luise und Tanja begleiten.

_____

6. Etwas ist in der Küche los.

_____

7. Meine Tante freute sich auf das Wiedersehen mit ihren Verwandten.

_____

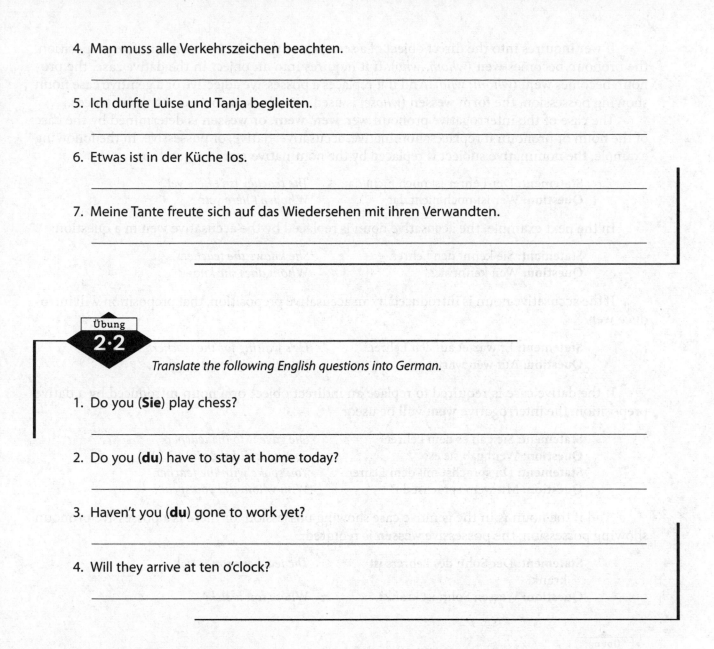

Übung

2·2

Translate the following English questions into German.

1. Do you (**Sie**) play chess?

_____

2. Do you (**du**) have to stay at home today?

_____

3. Haven't you (**du**) gone to work yet?

_____

4. Will they arrive at ten o'clock?

_____

Interrogative words

Interrogative words are used to pose a question about a specific element in a sentence: *who, what, when, where, how,* and so on. For the most part, German and English interrogative words are used in much the same way.

Wer

The interrogative **wer** (*who*) inquires into the person or persons mentioned in a statement. But **wer** is a singular pronoun and requires a singular conjugation of the verb, even when it inquires into a plural subject. For example:

Tina wohnt jetzt in Bremen.	*Tina lives in Bremen now.*
Wer wohnt jetzt in Bremen?	*Who lives in Bremen now?*
Meine Eltern waren im Harz.	*My parents were in the Harz Mountains.*
Wer war im Harz?	*Who was in the Harz Mountains?*

If **wer** inquires into the direct object of a sentence or the object of an accusative preposition, the pronoun becomes **wen** (*whom, who*). If it inquires into an object in the dative case, the pronoun becomes **wem** (*whom, who*). And if it replaces a possessive adjective or a genitive case noun showing possession, the form **wessen** (*whose*) is used. Let's look at some example sentences.

The case of the interrogative pronoun **wer, wen, wem,** or **wessen** is determined by the case of the noun or pronoun it replaces: nominative, accusative, dative, or possessive. In the following example, the nominative subject is replaced by the nominative **wer** in a question:

Statement: Der Lehrer ist noch nicht da.	*The teacher isn't here yet.*
Question: Wer ist noch nicht da?	*Who isn't here yet?*

In the next example, the accusative noun is replaced by the accusative **wen** in a question:

Statement: Sie kennt den Lehrer.	*She knows the teacher.*
Question: Wen kennt sie?	*Whom does she know?*

If the accusative noun is introduced by an accusative preposition, that preposition will introduce **wen**:

Statement: Er wartet auf den Lehrer.	*He's waiting for the teacher.*
Question: Auf wen wartet er?	*For whom is he waiting?*

If the dative case is required to replace an indirect object or a noun introduced by a dative preposition, the interrogative **wem** will be used:

Statement: Sie gab es dem Lehrer.	*She gave it to the teacher.*
Question: Wem gab sie es?	*To whom did she give it?*
Statement: Du sprachst mit dem Lehrer.	*You spoke with the teacher.*
Question: Mit wem sprachst du?	*With whom did you speak?*

And if the noun is in the genitive case showing possession, or there is a possessive pronoun showing possession, the possessive **wessen** is required:

Statement: Der Sohn des Lehrers ist krank.	*The teacher's son is sick.*
Question: Wessen Sohn ist krank?	*Whose son is sick?*

Übung
2·3

Rewrite the following sentences, changing the underlined word or phrase to the appropriate form: **wer**, **wen**, **wem**, *or* **wessen**.

EXAMPLE: <u>Er</u> kann uns gut verstehen.

    <u>Wer kann uns gut verstehen?</u>

1. Maria hatte ein Geschenk <u>für dich</u>.

   _____

2. Peter möchte <u>mit der neuen Studentin</u> tanzen.

   _____

3. Die Verwandten in Deutschland wollen <u>ihr</u> helfen.

   _____

4. Ihre Kinder werden mit Liebe erzogen.

_____

5. Sie möchten <u>mich</u> morgen besuchen.

_____

Was

The interrogative **was** (_what_) inquires into an object or group of objects in a sentence. It replaces the subject of the sentence or an accusative object. Its dative form is **wem**. Like **wer**, **was** is a singular pronoun.

The possessive form **wessen** is used to replace a possessive adjective or a genitive case noun showing possession.

Even if the noun or pronoun replaced by **was** is a plural, the verb in the question will have a singular conjugation:

> **Statement:** Diese Bücher sind alt.   _These books are old._
> **Question:** Was ist alt?   _What is old?_

When replacing a direct object, the pronoun **was** is again used:

> **Statement:** Er kauft eine neue Uhr.   _He buys a new clock._
> **Question:** Was kauft er?   _What does he buy?_

German sometimes uses an indirect object with non-human animates, a structure that would sound strange in English. To illustrate that point consider the following sentence and the question that follows:

> **Statement:** Der Schäfer scherte den   _The shepherd sheared the wool from the sheep._
> Schafen die Wolle.
> **Question:** Wem scherte der Schäfer die   _From what did the shepherd shear the wool?_
> Wolle?

The possessive **wessen** replaces the genitive case noun or possessive adjective in a question.

> **Statement:** Wir verkaufen die Wolle des   _We sell the sheep's wool._
> Schafs.
> **Question:** Wessen Wolle verkaufen wir?   _Whose wool do we sell?_

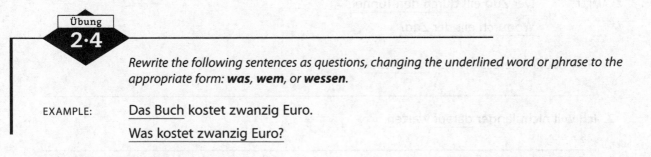

ÜBUNG
2·4

Rewrite the following sentences as questions, changing the underlined word or phrase to the appropriate form: **was**, **wem**, _or_ **wessen**.

EXAMPLE: <u>Das Buch</u> kostet zwanzig Euro.

                Was kostet zwanzig Euro?

1. Ich habe <u>es</u> im Schaufenster gesehen.

_____

2. Der Gerber wird <u>einem Tier</u> das Fell abziehen.

_____

3. Die Bauern ziehen <u>Schafe</u> auf.

_____

4. Die Nase <u>des Hundes</u> war sehr kalt.

_____

Prepositional adverbs

If an inanimate noun follows an accusative or dative preposition and you wish to replace that noun with a pronoun, a prepositional adverb is formed. In a statement, a prepositional adverb begins with **da(r)-** and ends with the preposition. In a question, it begins with **wo(r)-** and ends with the preposition. The **-r** is added before a preposition that begins with a vowel. For example:

Prepositional phrase: im Klassenzimmer	_in the classroom_
Prepositional adverb: darin, worin	_in it, in what_
Prepositional phrase: vor der Tür	_in front of the door_
Prepositional adverb: davor, wovor	_in front of it, in front of what_
Prepositional phrase: an der Wand	_at the wall_
Prepositional adverb: daran, woran	_at it, at what_

There is a tendency to use **um was** and to avoid using a prepositional adverb when saying _around what_.

Let's look at some example questions that include prepositional adverbs:

Worin sitzen sie?	_What are they sitting in?_
Worüber spricht Karl?	_What is Karl talking about?_
Worauf warte ich?	_What am I waiting for?_

Übung
2·5

Rewrite the following sentences as questions. Change the underlined word or phrase to the appropriate prepositional adverb needed for a question.

EXAMPLE: Der Zug eilt <u>durch den Tunnel</u>.

<u>Wodurch eilt der Zug?</u>

1. Herr Bauer interessiert sich <u>für Chemie</u>.

_____

2. Ich will nicht länger <u>darauf</u> warten.

_____

3. Der Lehrling hat nicht <u>von der neuen Methode</u> gehört.

_____

4. Die neuen Auswanderer sehnen sich danach.

   _____

5. Die Kinder spielten damit.

   _____

6. Ich habe meine Freunde um Hilfe gebeten.

   _____

7. Der Professor kämpfte gegen falsche Meinungen.

   _____

If the preposition **in**, **zu**, or **nach** is used to mean *to a place*, its interrogative form will be **wohin** (*where to, whither*). Do not form a prepositional adverb:

Wohin ging er?	*Where did he go?*
Wohin laufen sie?	*Where are they running (to)?*
Wohin reist sie?	*Where is she traveling (to)?*

If the prepositions **von** and **aus** are used to mean *from a place*, their interrogative form will be **woher** (*from where, whence*). Do not form a prepositional adverb:

Er kommt von der Arbeit.	*He's coming from work.*
Woher kommt er?	*Where is he coming from?*
Die Wanderer kamen aus dem Wald.	*The hikers came out of the woods.*
Woher kamen die Wanderer?	*Where did the hikers come from?*

Only **wer** and **was** are declined and used as pronouns. Other interrogative words are adverbial or are substitutes for modifiers. Some of the most commonly used ones are:

wann	*when*
was für	*what kind of* (plural)
was für ein	*what kind of a* (singular)
welcher	*which*
wie	*how*
wie viel(e)	*how much, many*
wo	*where* (location)

The interrogative phrase **was für (ein)** can be used with singular or plural nouns. Use **was für ein** with singular nouns and **was für** with plural nouns. For example:

Was für eine Katze hast du?	*What kind of a cat do you have?*
Was für Haustiere hast du?	*What kind of pets do you have?*

Let's look at some sentences that illustrate these interrogatives:

Statement: Der Zug kommt in zehn Minuten.	*The train comes in ten minutes.*
Question: Wann kommt der Zug?	*When does the train come?*

Warum is used to ask a question about an entire clause that begins with *because:*

Statement: Er spricht so laut, weil er taub ist.	*He speaks so loudly because he's deaf.*
Question: Warum spricht er so laut?	*Why does he speak so loudly?*

When using **was für ein**, the case of the article **ein** is determined by the usage of the noun it modifies and not by the preposition **für** that precedes **ein:**

Statement: Sie hat einen Rennwagen.	*She has a racing car.*
Question: Was für einen Wagen hat sie?	*What kind of a car does she have?*
Ein Lehrbuch liegt auf dem Tisch.	*A textbook is lying on the table.*
Was für ein Buch liegt auf dem Tisch?	*What kind of book is lying on the table?*

Use **welcher** to ask about the distinction between two people or things:

Statement: Der neue Student ist klug.	*The new student is smart.*
Question: Welcher Student ist klug?	*Which student is smart?*

Wie is generally used to ask *how* in a question, but it also occurs in commonly used idiomatic expressions such as in the following example:

Statement: Der Junge heißt Karl.	*The boy's name is Karl.*
Question: Wie heißt der Junge?	*What is the boy's name?*

Normally, **wie viel** is used with singular nouns (*how much*) and **wie viele** with plural nouns (*how many*). (However, **wie viel** is also often used in place of **wie viele**.)

Statement: Er hat zwei Hefte.	*He has two notebooks.*
Question: Wie viele Hefte hat er?	*How many notebooks does he have?*

The interrogative **wo** inquires into location and should not be confused with **wohin**, which inquires into direction or motion:

Statement: Sie arbeiten im Garten.	*They're working in the garden.*
Question: Wo arbeiten sie?	*Where are they working?*

In addition, there is a variety of other interrogative phrases formed with **wie**. For example:

wie alt	*how old*
wie groß	*how big*
wie oft	*how often*
wie schnell	*how fast*
wie weit	*how far*
um wie viel Uhr	*at what time*

Let's look at some sentences that illustrate the use of these interrogatives:

Statement: Karin ist vier Jahre alt.	*Karin is four years old.*
Question: Wie alt ist Karin?	*How old is Karin?*
Statement: Das Zimmer hat zehn Quadratmeter.	*The room is ten meters square.*
Question: Wie groß ist das Zimmer?	*How big is the room?*
Statement: Er geht alle vier Tage in die Stadt.	*He goes to the city every four days.*
Question: Wie oft geht er in die Stadt?	*How often does he go to the city?*

In general, interrogative words are followed by the regular word order for a question:

interrogative word + verb + subject + ?
Wann + kommt + der Zug + ?
When is the train arriving?

Übung
2·6

*Rewrite each sentence as a question using the underlined word or phrase as the cue for determining which interrogative word to use: **wann**, **warum**, **was für (ein)**, **welcher**, **wie**, or **wo**.*

EXAMPLE: Sie wohnen jetzt <u>in Leipzig</u>.

<u>Wo wohnen sie jetzt?</u>

1. Der Rechtsanwalt sprach <u>zu laut</u>.

_____

2. Die junge Dame hat einen <u>teuren</u> Pullover gekauft.

_____

3. Du musst einen Mantel tragen, <u>denn es ist heute sehr kalt</u>.

_____

4. <u>Der ältere</u> Junge ist ziemlich dumm.

_____

5. Seine Tochter studiert <u>an der Universität Hamburg</u>.

_____

Übung
2·7

*Rewrite each sentence as a question using the underlined word or phrase as the cue for determining which interrogative word to use: **wie alt**, **wie groß**, **wie oft**, or **wie viel**.*

EXAMPLE: Sie hat <u>zehn</u> neue Blusen.

<u>Wie viele neue Blusen hat sie?</u>

1. Unser Schlafzimmer hat <u>nur achtzehn Quadratmeter</u>.

_____

2. Onkel Peter hat <u>ein paar</u> Nelken gekauft.

_____

3. Doktor Schmidt wird am elften Dezember <u>achtzig</u> werden.

_____

Compose questions using the words provided in each list. Add any necessary words.

EXAMPLE: kommen / er / mit / Freund / nach Hause / ?

<u>Kommt er mit einem Freund nach Hause?</u>

1. was / fallen / von / Dach / auf / Straße / ?

_____

2. klettern / Bergsteiger / den steilen Felsen / hinauf / ?

_____

3. mit / wer / haben / du / so lange / tanzen / ?

_____

4. wie lange / müssen / ihr / in / Hauptstadt / auf / euer / Zug / warten / ?

_____

5. können / du / mich / zu / Bahnhof / begleiten / ?

_____

6. welcher / Geschäft / haben / beste / Preise / ?

_____

7. durch / schützen / man / Pflanzen / vor / Kälte / des Winters / ?

_____

Write original sentences. Begin each one with the cue words provided.

EXAMPLE: (was)

Was siehst du im Garten?

1. (was für ein)

_____

2. (auf wen)

_____

3. (worauf)

_____

4. (wohin)

_____

Questions and answers

In the previous chapter you encountered the varieties of interrogative forms that exist in German. In this chapter you will have an opportunity to apply that knowledge as you analyze the elements of sentences and determine what kinds of questions to ask and what kinds of answers to give.

Let's look at an English sentence and the kinds of questions that can be formed from the words in it:

> *Every day the children's voices grew louder and louder, because Grandpa always played his radio so loudly.*

The following questions can be asked of the various elements in this sentence:

> *How often did the children's voices grow louder and louder?*
> *Whose voices grew louder and louder every day?*
> *What grew louder and louder every day?*
> *Did the children's voices grow louder and louder every day?*
> *Did the children's voices grow quieter and quieter every day?*
> *How did the children's voices grow every day?*
> *Why did the children's voices grow louder and louder every day?*
> *Who always played his radio so loudly?*
> *How often did Grandpa play his radio so loudly?*
> *What did Grandpa always play so loudly?*
> *Did Grandpa always play his radio so loudly?*
> *Did Grandpa ever play his radio quietly?*
> *Whose radio did Grandpa always play so loudly?*
> *What happened every day as a result of Grandpa always playing his radio so loudly?*

In the same way, a German sentence can be separated into these kinds of sentence elements, and questions can be formed about them as well. Knowing how to do this effectively will help you to write better sentences.

Too often, learners assume that there are only a couple of questions to be derived from a sentence. But, in fact, nearly each word in a sentence can serve as a cue for a question. Let's look at a simple example first:

Seine Geschwister lebten in Darmstadt bei der Tante eines Freundes.	*His brothers and sisters lived in Darmstadt with the aunt of a friend.*

Now let's look at the questions you can ask. Some can inquire into the subject of the sentence and the words that modify it:

Wessen Geschwister lebten in Darmstadt bei der Tante eines Freundes?	*Whose brothers and sisters lived in Darmstadt with the aunt of a friend?*
Wer lebte in Darmstadt bei der Tante eines Freundes?	*Who lived in Darmstadt with the aunt of a friend?*
Lebten seine Eltern in Darmstadt bei der Tante eines Freundes?	*Did his parents live in Darmstadt with the aunt of a friend?*

Some questions will ask about location:

Wo lebten seine Geschwister?	*Where did his brothers and sisters live?*
Bei wem lebten seine Geschwister in Darmstadt?	*With whom did his brothers and sisters live in Darmstadt?*
Lebten seine Geschwister in Berlin bei der Tante eines Freundes?	*Did his brothers and sisters live in Berlin with the aunt of a friend?*

Some questions seek to distinguish between two persons or things by inquiring *which* or *what*:

In welcher Stadt lebten seine Geschwister?	*In what city did his brothers and sisters live?*

Some questions ask *whose* to identify a person or thing or to show ownership:

Bei wessen Tante lebten seine Geschwister in Darmstadt?	*With whose aunt did his brothers and sisters live in Darmstadt?*

Some **ja-nein** questions seek to clarify information in the sentence:

Lebten seine Geschwister in Darmstadt bei dem Onkel eines Freundes?	*Did his brothers and sisters live in Darmstadt with the uncle of a friend?*
Lebten seine Geschwister in Darmstadt bei der Tante einer Freundin?	*Did his brothers and sisters live in Darmstadt with the aunt of a girlfriend?*

When you merely invert the subject and verb, you are asking a general question about all the information in the sentence, and this type of question will require a **ja-nein** answer:

Lebten seine Geschwister in Darmstadt bei der Tante eines Freundes?	*Did his brothers and sisters live in Darmstadt with the aunt of a friend?*

As you can see, at least eleven questions were able to be derived from a sentence composed of ten words. When you are able to do this on your own, you will have the skill to understand the complexities of a sentence and how to compose your own sentences more accurately.

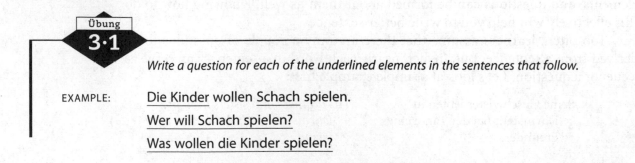

Übung
3·1

Write a question for each of the underlined elements in the sentences that follow.

EXAMPLE: Die Kinder wollen Schach spielen.

Wer will Schach spielen?

Was wollen die Kinder spielen?

1. Unser Lehrer wird nach Irak fahren.

    a. _____

    b. _____

2. Der Kieler Kanal verbindet die Nordsee mit der Ostsee.

    a. _____

    b. _____

3. Sie bringen den Kanarienvogel zum Tierarzt.

    a. _____

    b. _____

4. Das große Wörterbuch kostet vierzig Euro.

    a. _____

    b. _____

5. Der alte Herr trägt immer einen alten Hut.

    a. _____

    b. _____

6. In den Hauptstraßen einer Großstadt gibt es viele interessante Geschäfte.

    a. _____

    b. _____

7. Der Polizist brachte den verhafteten Dieb zum Polizeiamt.

    a. _____

    b. _____

Übung
3·2

Write an appropriate answer to each of the following questions.

1. Sind gute Sprachkenntnisse jedem Menschen nützlich?

    _____

2. Wer machte dem Kranken große Hoffnungen?

    _____

3. Warum müssen die Touristen die deutsche Sprache lernen?

    _____

4. Woher kommen Sie?

    _____

5. Wessen Vetter aus Amerika war letzten Sommer hier?

   _____

6. Wie arbeitet der Student?

   _____

7. Wodurch erfuhr sie das Unglück?

   _____

8. Für wen soll der Vater sorgen?

   _____

9. Wen liebt die Mutter am meisten?

   _____

10. Woraus trinkt man Tee oder Kaffee?

    _____

Wer and was

You are already aware that the interrogative pronouns **wer** and **was** are used for questions regarding people and things, respectively. Since these pronouns can be declined, the answers to questions that use these words require the use of the same case as the interrogative pronoun. That is, the answer to **wer** will be a nominative case pronoun or noun such as **die Frau**, and the answer to **wen** will be an accusative case pronoun or noun such as **den Mann**.

The declension of **wer** and **was**:

Nominative:	wer	was
Accusative:	wen	was
Dative:	wem	wem
Genitive (Possessive):	wessen	wessen

Remember that the accusative and dative forms of **was** are not used after prepositions. Instead, a prepositional adverb is formed, for example: **wofür** (*for what*) or **wovon** (*from what*).

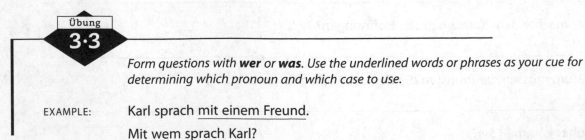

Übung

3·3

Form questions with **wer** or **was**. Use the underlined words or phrases as your cue for determining which pronoun and which case to use.

EXAMPLE: Karl sprach <u>mit einem Freund</u>.

             <u>Mit wem sprach Karl?</u>

1. Die Kinder müssen sich die Hände und Gesichter waschen.

   _____

2. Ein weißer Storch kreiste über dem kleinen Dorf.

   _____

3. Die Gäste fragen nach seiner kranken Frau.

   _____

4. Sie mussten zwei Stunden auf ihn warten.

   _____

5. Wilhelm hat sich in Klaudia verliebt.

   _____

6. Es gelingt ihr nicht, die Aufgabe zu lösen.

   _____

7. Er muss zehn Schafen die Wolle scheren.

   _____

8. Ich kann dir nicht glauben.

   _____

9. Der Tod ihres besten Schülers betrübt die Lehrerin.

   _____

10. Es freut uns, dass du kommst.

    _____

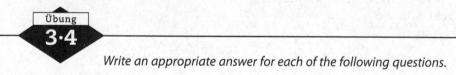

Übung 3·4

Write an appropriate answer for each of the following questions.

1. Wen tadelt der Vater?

   _____

2. Durch welches Land wollen sie eine Reise machen?

   _____

3. Wer liebt es nicht, nach dem Essen zu rauchen?

   _____

4. Worüber freuten sich die Eltern?

   _____

5. Was ist nicht möglich?

_____

6. Wem gehören diese Handschuhe?

_____

7. Wessen Wagen hat Herr Schäfer reparieren lassen?

_____

8. Was wird der Fahrer auf die Straße schieben?

_____

9. Womit fahren Sie ins Ausland?

_____

10. Bei wem musste die arme Frau wohnen?

_____

In summary, interrogative words other than **wer** and **was** form questions about adverbial or adjectival expressions: *when, why, where, how,* and so forth. And if those expressions include a preposition, a prepositional adverb is formed. But remember that prepositional phrases that describe *location, motion to a place,* or *motion from a place* require the use of **wo, wohin,** and **woher,** respectively:

- Location (*Where?*):

    wo + verb of location + subject + ?
    Wo + sitzt + er + ?
    Where is he sitting?

- Motion to a place (*Where to?*):

    wohin + verb of motion + subject + ?
    Wohin + geht + er + ?
    Where is he going?

- Motion from a place (*Where from?*):

    woher + verb of motion + subject + ?
    Woher + kommst + du + ?
    Where do you come from?

If the verb alone is the target of a question, no interrogative word is required. The verb merely precedes the subject in the question:

Er lernt Deutsch.	*He is learning German.*
Lernt er Deutsch?	*Is he learning German?*

Form questions by using the underlined words or phrases as your cues for determining which interrogative word to use.

EXAMPLE: Karl war gestern in Bremen.

Wann war Karl in Bremen?

1. Er kommt ziemlich oft spät zur Schule.

_____

2. Die Kinder dürfen nicht im Park spielen, weil es sehr kalt ist.

_____

3. Meine Nichte hat mit ihren Freundinnen einen Ausflug gemacht.

_____

4. Die alte Dame trug ein altmodisches Abendkleid.

_____

5. Der süße kleine Junge singt wie ein Engel.

_____

6. Der Fremdenführer will den Besuchern die schönen Gemälde zeigen.

_____

7. Ihr erster Sohn ist am zwanzigsten Mai geboren.

_____

8. Seine Tochter tanzt so schön wie eine Ballerina.

_____

9. Das Kind spielt sehr gut Geige.

_____

10. In diesem Restaurant darf man nicht rauchen.

_____

Write an appropriate answer to each of the following questions.

1. Was darf man in der Kirche nicht machen?

_____

2. Wo sollst du deine Freunde erwarten?

_____

3. Warum liegt der Mann den ganzen Tag im Bett?

_____

4. Was für einen Schlips soll ich tragen?

_____

5. Wie haben sie vom Tod ihres Großvaters erfahren?

_____

6. Wofür interessiert sich die Studentin?

_____

7. Wohin laufen diese Leute?

_____

8. Was für Geschenke haben Sie gekauft?

_____

9. Wann ist ihr Geburtstag?

_____

10. Wen suchen die weinenden Kinder?

_____

Compose questions using the words provided in each list. Add any necessary words. Then answer the questions appropriately.

EXAMPLE: kommen / er / mit / Amerikaner / nach Hause / ?

Kommt er mit einem Amerikaner nach Hause?

Nein, er kommt mit einem Ausländer nach Hause.

1. warum / spielen / du / nicht / mit / andere / Kinder / ?

a. _____

b. _____

2. woher / haben / er / dies / alt / Bücher / bekommen / ?

a. _____

b. _____

3. wie viel / Meter / Stoff / haben / Frau Benz / brauchen / ?

a. _____

b. _____

4. wie oft / sein / ihr / Ausland / reisen / ?

a. _____

b. _____

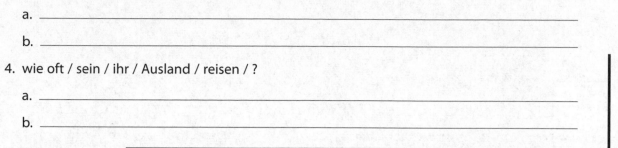

Übung

3·8

Compose original questions using the words in parentheses as your cues. Then answer each question.

EXAMPLE: (was)

Was haben Sie gekauft?

Ich habe einen neuen BMW gekauft.

1. (wann)

a. _____

b. _____

2. (warum)

a. _____

b. _____

3. (wie lange)

a. _____

b. _____

4. (wohin)

a. _____

b. _____

Imperatives

·4·

Imperatives are commands given, for the most part, to the second person pronoun *you*. In English, the infinitive of a verb without the particle word *to* is used to give a casual command and the same form with the addition of the word *please* is used to give a more formal or polite command:

> *Sit down.*   *Sit down, please.*   *Sign here.*   *Sign here, please.*

German is similar but not identical. For one thing, German has three forms for the pronoun *you*: **du**, **ihr**, and **Sie**. Therefore, there are three imperative forms that correspond to the usual uses of those three pronouns: informal singular, informal plural, and formal singular or plural, respectively:

> **du** imperative + predicate → command
> **ihr** imperative + predicate → command
> **Sie** imperative + predicate → command

With many German verbs, the stem of the verb becomes the stem of the imperative form. The stem of a verb is the infinitive minus the **-(e)n** ending (**machen – mach**). The **du**-form adds an **-e** to the stem, the **ihr**-form adds a **-t**, and the **Sie**-form adds an **-en** and is paired with the pronoun **Sie**. Look at the following examples:

	DU	IHR	SIE	
lachen	lache!	lacht!	lachen Sie!	*laugh*
kaufen	kaufe!	kauft!	kaufen Sie!	*buy*
warten	warte!	wartet!	warten Sie!	*wait*

The **-e** ending of the **du**-form is optional for most verbs. However, if the stem of the verb ends in **-d** or **-t** the ending is not optional and must be retained:

	DU	IHR	SIE	
stellen	stell(e)!	stellt!	stellen Sie!	*put*
senden	sende!	sendet!	senden Sie!	*broadcast*
streiten	streite!	streitet!	streiten Sie!	*quarrel*

If a verb requires an umlaut in the second and third persons singular in the present tense conjugations, for example, **tragen—trägst**, **trägt** (*to carry*), the imperative forms follow the pattern above and the umlaut is not used:

- ◆ **Du** imperative:

    verb stem(e) + **!**
    Schlag(e) + !
    Hit!

- ◆ **Ihr** imperative:

    verb stem + **-t** + **!**
    Schlagt + !
    Hit!

- ◆ **Sie** imperative:

    verb stem + **-en** + **Sie** + **!**
    Schlagen + Sie + !
    Hit!

But if a verb forms its singular second and third persons present tense conjugations with a vowel shift to **-i-** or **-ie-**, the **du**-form of the imperative is formed from the second person present tense conjugation (**du**) minus the **-st** ending and never adds an **-e** ending. The other two forms follow the previous pattern. For example:

geben	gib!	gebt!	geben Sie!	*give*
helfen	hilf!	helft!	helfen Sie!	*help*
sehen	sieh!	seht!	sehen Sie!	*see*

A notable exception to this rule is **werden**:

werden	werde!	werdet!	werden Sie!	*become*

The only verb that has its own imperative pattern is **sein**. It forms the imperative from the infinitive:

sein	sei!	seid!	seien Sic!	*be*

Inseparable and separable prefixes act the same way in an imperative sentence as they do in any other sentence:

besuchen	besuche!	besucht!	besuchen Sie!	*visit*
zuhören	hör zu!	hört zu!	hören Sie zu!	*listen*

Note that imperatives are punctuated with an exclamation point in German.

Übung
4·1

*Rewrite each of the following infinitives as imperatives appropriate for **du**, **ihr**, and **Sie**.*

	DU	IHR	SIE
1. trinken	_____	_____	_____
2. anstellen	_____	_____	_____

3. tun   _____   _____   _____

4. brechen   _____   _____   _____

5. empfehlen   _____   _____   _____

6. abfahren   _____   _____   _____

7. lesen   _____   _____   _____

8. nehmen   _____   _____   _____

9. essen   _____   _____   _____

10. stehlen   _____   _____   _____

Übung 4·2

Using the word or phrase in parentheses as your cue, write an appropriate **du-**, **ihr-**, or **Sie-**form command with the infinitive provided.

EXAMPLE: (Kind) gehen   <u>Geh zur Schule!</u>

1. (Mutter und Vater) helfen _____

2. (Doktor Schmidt) essen _____

3. (Richter) schreiben _____

4. (Arzt und Pflegerin) besuchen _____

5. (Bruder) sein _____

6. (Hund) fressen _____

7. (Freund) einladen _____

8. (Tochter) werden _____

9. (Kinder) antworten _____

10. (Touristen) aussteigen _____

Addressing groups

There is another form of imperative that is used when a command is not directed at any particular individual and is meant to give information to people at large instead. These imperatives can be heard over loudspeakers or read on signs in public places. Their formation is quite simple: The infinitive is used as the imperative form and is usually found at the end of the phrase. For example:

Den Rasen nicht betreten!	*Keep off the grass.*
Nicht rauchen!	*No smoking.*
Gepäck aufmachen!	*Open (your) baggage.*

Change the following infinitives to imperatives that address people in general. The information in parentheses tells where the action takes place. Add any necessary words.

EXAMPLE: aufmachen (*at the border*)

Gepäck aufmachen!

1. zurückbleiben (*on the platform as a train arrives*)

   _____

2. anfassen (*a sign on a museum exhibit*)

   _____

3. anstellen (*an announcement about where to line up*)

   _____

4. aussteigen (*an announcement to get off the streetcar*)

   _____

Imperatives with wir

Most commands are given to the second person pronoun *you*. But in both English and German it is possible to include yourself in the command and thereby make it seem a bit more polite. In fact, it sounds more like a suggestion than an imperative. In English, this is done by beginning a verb phrase with *let's*:

> *Let's get something to eat.*   *Let's leave soon.*

The German version of this type of command is equally simple. The present tense conjugation of a verb in the first person plural (**wir**) with the verb preceding the pronoun is all that is required:

> Essen wir im italienischen Restaurant!   *Let's eat at an Italian restaurant.*
> Kaufen wir einen neuen Wagen!   *Let's buy a new car.*
> Fahren wir jetzt ab!   *Let's leave now.*

> **verb + wir + complement + !**
> Gehen + wir + nach Hause + !
> *Let's go home.*

A similar expression is formed by using the verb **lassen** (*to let*). It can include the speaker or not, as we shall see below, but must conform, regardless, to the second person pronoun required by the circumstances: informal or formal, singular or plural. Therefore, a distinction is made among the **du-**, **ihr-**, and **Sie**-forms. First, let us look at the basic imperative, meaning *let*, not *let's* (i.e., not including the speaker). For example:

> Lass ihn ausreden! (du)   *Let him finish speaking.*
> Lasst die Kinder spielen! (ihr)   *Let the children play.*
> Lassen Sie sie warten! (Sie)   *Let them wait.*

lass/lasst/lassen Sie + object + infinitive + !
Lassen Sie + ihn + mitkommen + !
Let him come along.

If you add the accusative pronoun **uns** (*us*) to the equation, you have once again a form that means *let's*. For example:

Lass uns nicht mehr streiten! (du)	*Let's not quarrel anymore.*
Lasst uns bald gehen! (ihr)	*Let's go soon.*
Lassen Sie uns darüber sprechen! (Sie)	*Let's talk about it.*

lass uns/lasst uns/lassen Sie uns + complement + !
Lass uns + jetzt gehen + !
Let's go now.

Übung
4·4

*Rewrite the following sentences as imperatives with **wir**. Careful: The sentences provided are in a variety of tenses.*

EXAMPLE: Er ging schnell nach Hause.

Gehen wir schnell nach Hause!

1. Die Freunde segelten in den Hafen.

   _____

2. Die Frau ist am Marktplatz eingestiegen.

   _____

3. Sie aßen im Schnellimbiss.

   _____

4. Sie liest die amerikanischen Zeitungen.

   _____

5. Ihr seid nicht um die Ecke gefahren.

   _____

6. Er legte die Kinder aufs Bett.

   _____

7. Ich muss einen Polizisten fragen, wo die Bank ist.

   _____

*Rewrite each sentence with **lassen** to form an imperative that begins with the meaning* let. *Conjugate **lassen** for the pronoun **du**. Then rewrite the imperative changing the direct object to **uns** and thereby the meaning of the verb to* let's.

EXAMPLE: Martin spricht darüber.

Lass Martin darüber sprechen!

Lass uns darüber sprechen!

1. Sie schlafen morgen aus.

   a. _____

   b. _____

2. Er ißt den letzten Apfel.

   a. _____

   b. _____

3. Er schwimmt nicht im kalten Fluss.

   a. _____

   b. _____

*Follow the same directions, but conjugate **lassen** for **ihr** instead of **du**.*

4. Die Mädchen spielen mit den Kindern.

   a. _____

   b. _____

5. Er besucht die neue Kunsthalle.

   a. _____

   b. _____

*Follow the same directions, but conjugate **lassen** for **Sie** instead of **du**.*

6. Sie fängt um achtzehn Uhr an.

   a. _____

   b. _____

7. Herr Bauer kehrt in die Heimat zurück.

   a. _____

   b. _____

Write original imperative sentences. Use the cues in parentheses to tell you whether to use a **du-***,* **ihr-***, or* **Sie**-*form conjugation. Also conform to the type of imperative indicated: a direct second person command or a command with* **lassen***.*

A direct second person command:

1. (Professor Kaufmann)

_____

2. (Brüder)

_____

3. (Tante und Onkel)

_____

4. (Pfarrer)

_____

A command with **lassen***, with or without* **uns***:*

5. (Freundinnen)

_____

6. (Polizist)

_____

7. (Herr Kamps und Frau Schäfter)

_____

Coordinating conjunctions

The main clause of a German sentence contains a subject and a verb and makes complete sense when it stands alone. Except when some element other than the subject begins a main clause, the subject precedes the verb:

Er kommt spät nach Hause.	*He comes home late.*
Tina versteht es nicht.	*Tina doesn't understand it.*
Setz dich hin! (**Du** *is understood.*)	*Sit down.*

This word order is important when using coordinating conjunctions.

Coordinating conjunctions

Coordinating conjunctions can link together words, phrases, or even complete sentences (main clauses):

word + conjunction + word
phrase + conjunction + phrase
clause + conjunction + clause

The most commonly used coordinating conjunctions are:

aber	*but*
denn	*because, for, since*
oder	*or*
sondern (*used with* **nicht** *or* **kein**)	*but (rather)*
und	*and*

When combining sentences with these conjunctions, a comma is used to mark off the two clauses. With **und** and sometimes with **aber**, however, this is optional. If the combination of two clauses with **und** is confusing, a comma can precede **und** for the sake of clarity.

Let's look at some example sentences that illustrate the use of coordinating conjunctions:

Der Mann klopfte laut an die Tür, aber niemand war zu Hause.	*The man knocked loudly on the door, but no one was home.*
Sie ging nicht zur Schule, denn sie war wieder krank.	*She didn't go to school, because she was sick again.*
Du darfst hier übernachten, oder wir können ein Hotel für dich finden.	*You can stay here overnight, or we can find a hotel for you.*

Ich habe keinen Artikel gefunden, sondern ich habe ein ganzes Buch über sein Leben gekauft.	*I didn't find an article, but I bought a whole book about his life.*
Vater schläft auf dem Sofa und Mutter arbeitet in der Küche.	*Father is sleeping on the sofa, and mother is working in the kitchen.*

sentence 1 + comma + coordinating conjunction + sentence 2
Er bleibt zu Hause + , + denn + er ist krank.
He's staying home, because he's sick.

When the subject of the first clause is identical to the subject of the second clause, it is possible to omit the second subject and sometimes even the verb. For example:

Wir können bei Inge übernachten, oder ein Hotel finden.	*We can stay overnight at Inge's or find a hotel.*
Vater kann nicht schlafen und arbeitet in der Küche.	*Father can't sleep and is working in the kitchen.*

This is especially true of **sondern**:

Erik ist nicht eingeschlafen, sondern hat die ganze Nacht an Tina gedacht.	*Erik didn't fall asleep but rather thought about Tina all night.*
Ich habe keinen Artikel gefunden, sondern ein ganzes Buch über sein Leben gekauft.	*I didn't find an article but bought a whole book about his life.*

These five conjunctions are unique in that they require no word order change. The standard word order for a declarative, interrogative, or imperative sentence is used in both clauses that surround a coordinating conjunction.

Übung
5·1

Combine the following pairs of sentences with the appropriate conjunction. Choose the conjunction from the two provided in parentheses for each set.

EXAMPLE: (und / oder) Werner ist mein Freund. Tina ist meine Freundin.

Werner ist mein Freund und Tina ist meine Freundin.

1. (aber / denn) Er wollte Tennis spielen. Das Wetter war endlich gut.

_____

2. (oder / sondern) Ich habe es nicht verloren. Ich habe es hinter dem Schrank versteckt.

_____

3. (und / denn) Paul studiert in Berlin. Er wohnt in einem Studentenheim.

_____

4. (oder / aber) Sei ruhig! Geh sofort nach Hause!

_____

5. (und / oder) Soll er einen roten Wagen kaufen? Soll er einen blauen Wagen kaufen?

_____

6. (und / aber) Ich höre was du sagst. Ich verstehe dich nicht.

_____

7. (sondern / und) Angela spielt Gitarre. Ihr Bruder spielt Flöte.

_____

Übung
5·2

Rewrite the following sentences by changing the underlined clause to an alternate clause that conforms to the meaning of the rest of the sentence.

EXAMPLE:　　Sie geht einkaufen, aber Peter bleibt zu Hause.

　　　　　　Sie geht einkaufen, aber ihre Schwester will eine Freundin besuchen.

1. Sie versuchte ihn zu warnen, aber der Junge hat sie nicht gehört.

_____

2. Die Studentin konnte nicht arbeiten, denn der Lärm war zu groß.

_____

3. Normalerweise ist der Herbst am schönsten, aber dieses Jahr ist der Winter wunderschön.

_____

4. Karl ist nicht zum Café gegangen, sondern ist wieder zu Hause geblieben.

_____

5. Der Schüler setzte sich auf seinen Platz und schrieb die Wörter in sein Heft.

_____

6. Im Schaufenster stehen große Puppen, aber sie sehen alt und schmutzig aus.

_____

7. Der Junge lernt das Gedicht nicht, sondern er sieht den ganzen Abend fern.

_____

8. Der Bauer sät das Korn und seine Frau pflegt den Gemüsegarten.

_____

9. Im Kühlschrank gibt es keinen Wein mehr, sondern nur ein paar Flaschen Bier.

   _____

10. Ich habe ihm mit Interesse zugehört, aber ich habe ihm kein Wort geglaubt.

    _____

Übung
5·3

Compose sentences using the words provided in each list. Add any necessary words.

EXAMPLE: morgen / kommen / er / mit / Freund / nach Hause
             <u>Morgen kommt er mit einem Freund nach Hause.</u>

1. tun / mir / Gefallen / und / mitkommen / !

   _____

2. Junge / müssen / gehorchen / oder / er / haben / Folgen / selbst / zu tragen

   _____

3. Kirschen / schmecken / sehr / gut / aber / wie viel / kosten / sie / ?

   _____

4. wir / machen / kein / Pause / sondern / arbeiten / bis / spät / in / Nacht

   _____

Übung
5·4

Write an original sentence with each of the coordinating conjunctions given.

1. aber

   _____

2. denn

   _____

3. oder

   _____

4. sondern

   _____

Subordinating conjunctions

·6·

There are many subordinating conjunctions, and they all share two characteristics: (1) they introduce dependent clauses that do not make complete sense when they stand alone; and (2) the conjugated verb in such clauses is normally the last element in the clause:

> **main clause + subordinating conjunction + dependent clause + verb**
> Ich besuchte Karl, + als + ich in der Hauptstadt + war.
> *I visited Karl when I was in the capital.*

Using subordinating conjunctions

Some of the most commonly used subordinating conjunctions are:

als	*when*	ob	*whether, if*
als ob (als wenn)	*as if*	obwohl	*although*
bevor	*before*	seit(dem)	*since*
bis	*until, by the time*	sobald	*as soon as*
da	*since*	sooft	*as often as*
damit	*so that*	soviel	*as far as*
dass	*that*	während	*while*
ehe	*before*	weil	*because*
falls	*in case*	wenn	*when(ever), if*
nachdem	*after*	wie	*as*

Let's look at a few example sentences. Take note of where the conjugated verb stands in the dependent clause:

Ich weiß, dass du lügst.	*I know that you're lying.*
Er konnte nicht einkaufen gehen, weil er pleite ist.	*He couldn't go shopping, because he's broke.*
Als sie in Paris war, kaufte sie sich ein paar neue Kleider.	*When she was in Paris, she bought a couple new dresses.*

Notice that in the first two example sentences above, the dependent clause is the second clause. In the third example, the dependent clause is the first clause. These clauses function in the same way no matter what their position in the sentence.

Whatever tense the verb is in, the conjugated verb or auxiliary will be the last element of a clause introduced by a subordinating conjunction:

..., dass er krank ist.	*. . . that he's sick.*
..., dass wir nichts gehört haben.	*. . . that we didn't hear anything.*
..., dass ich gut singen kann.	*. . . that I can sing well.*

There is only one exception to that rule. When a double infinitive structure is part of the sentence introduced by a subordinating conjunction, the auxiliary verb will precede the double infinitive. This occurs, of course, with modal auxiliaries and certain other verbs such as **helfen**, **hören**, **lassen**, and **sehen** (*to help, to hear, to get* or *to have done, to see*). With modal auxiliaries, for example:

..., weil sie uns wird einladen müssen.	*. . . , because she will have to invite us.*
..., weil er mit dir hatte fahren wollen.	*. . . , because he had wanted to drive with you.*

The same kind of word order occurs with **helfen**, **hören**, **lassen**, and **sehen**. For example:

..., weil Tina mir wird kochen helfen.	*. . . , because Tina will help me cook.*
..., weil ich es habe reparieren lassen.	*. . . , because I have had it repaired.*

When as a conjunction

You need to consider the conjunction *when* carefully. Although English uses the same conjunction for three different functions, German does not. There are three distinct German words, one for each function.

When using *when* to ask a question, the German interrogative is **wann**:

Wann kommen die Gäste morgen?	*When are the guests coming tomorrow?*
Bis wann kann ich vorbeikommen?	*Until what time can I drop by?*
Seit wann wohnt Lukas in Bremen?	*How long has Lukas been living in Bremen?*

The brief response to a **wann**-question can include **wann**:

Ich weiß nicht wann.	*I don't know when.*

In general, however, responses to a **wann**-question in the present tense require **wenn**:

Wann sind die Straßen naß?	*When are the streets wet?*
Die Straßen sind naß, wenn es regnet.	*The streets are wet when it rains.*

When using *when* to mean *whenever*, the German conjunction is again **wenn**, a subordinating conjunction:

Wenn wir nach Bonn kommen, besuchen wir unsere Tante.	*When(ever) we come to Bonn, we visit our aunt.*
Wenn Sie sich erst einmal eingearbeitet haben, werden Sie unsere Ziele besser verstehen.	*When you've had a chance to get used to the job, you'll understand our goals better.*
Wenn es Sommer wird, schwimmen wir jeden Tag.	*When summer comes, we'll go swimming every day.*

When using *when* in a past tense sentence, the German conjunction is **als**, also a subordinating conjunction:

Als er ankam, sah er Maria vor dem Haus stehen.	*When he arrived, he saw Maria standing in front of the house.*
Es fing an zu regnen, als wir zum Garten gehen wollten.	*It began to rain when we wanted to go to the garden.*
Gerade als Erik hier war, wurde meine Schwester krank.	*Just when Erik was here, my sister got sick.*

Comma usage with subordinating conjunctions

When two clauses are combined by a subordinating conjunction, the two clauses are separated by a comma:

Luise versteht, dass Benno zu Hause bleiben muss.

Luise understands that Benno has to stay home.

The two forms of sentence formation with subordinating conjunctions are:

main clause + subordinating conjunction + clause with verb in final position
Er besuchte sie, + als + er in Berlin war.
He visited her when he was in Berlin.

subordinating conjunction + clause with verb in final position + main clause
Als + er in Berlin war, + besuchte er sie.
When he was in Berlin, he visited her.

Remember that the verb will precede the subject in the main clause if the sentence is introduced by a subordinating conjunction as illustrated in the previous example.

Übung 6·1

*Fill in each blank with the missing word: **wann**, **wenn**, or **als**.*

1. _____ legt er sich ins Bett?

2. Sie musste das Studium aufgeben, _____ ihr Vater starb.

3. _____ ich die Universität verließ, traf ich einen Freund.

4. Man geht zum Arzt, _____ man krank ist.

5. _____ hat man Husten und Schnupfen?

6. _____ er im letzten Jahr in Kiel war, begegnete er einem

   Schulkameraden.

7. _____ die Kinder sechs Jahre alt sind, kommen sie in die Grundschule.

Übung 6·2

Complete each sentence with any appropriate phrase.

EXAMPLE: Er starb, als _____ .
             Er starb, als er im Krankenhaus war.

1. Wenn du nach Berlin reist, _____ .

2. Wenn _____ , dürfen Sie vorbeikommen.

3. Als die Touristen Südamerika besuchten, _____ .

4. Herr Schneider trifft einen Bekannten, wenn _____.

5. Wenn du isst, _____.

6. Wenn _____, denken die Kinder an Weihnachten.

7. _____, gehst du oft ins Theater?

Übung
6·3

*Fill in each blank with an appropriate subordinating conjunction. Do not use **wann**, **wenn**, or **als**.*

1. _____ wir im Ruhrgebiet waren, besuchten wir viele Fabriken.

2. _____ Herr Bauer starb, schrieb er sein Testament.

3. _____ wir abfahren, müssen wir die Koffer packen.

4. _____ sie meine Schwester war, wollte ich ihr kein Geld leihen.

5. Wissen Sie, _____ das Rathaus weit ist?

6. Wir kommen morgen vorbei, _____ wir genug Zeit haben.

7. Fahren wir zum Bahnhof mit einem Taxi, _____ wir den Zug erreichen!

8. _____ wir wissen, ist sie wieder schwanger.

9. Sie können mit uns reiten, _____ Sie wollen.

10. Ich kann nicht warten, _____ er zurückkommt.

11. _____ er zur Party ging, kämmte er sich wieder die Haare.

12. Ich habe ihnen geholfen, _____ ich konnte.

13. _____ Lukas betrunken war, wollte sie nicht mit ihm tanzen.

14. Hast du gewusst, _____ du den letzten Bus verpasst hast?

Übung
6·4

Complete each sentence with any appropriate phrase.

EXAMPLE: Er starb, ehe _____.
             Er starb, ehe er sein Testament schrieb.

1. Obwohl _____, verstand ich es nicht.

2. Während _____, haben sie oft Schach gespielt.

3. Er musste wieder zu Fuß gehen, weil _____.

4. Erik fragte uns, ob _____.

5. Sie haben nichts bezahlt, solange _____.

6. Kinder, wartet hier, bis _____!

7. Ich habe keine Ahnung, wie _____.

8. Beeilt euch, damit _____!

9. _____ er müde war, wollte er nach Hause gehen.

10. Obwohl _____, will ich nicht Skilaufen gehen.

11. Seitdem _____, ist sie nie zu Hause.

12. Nachdem er sich den Finger verletzt hatte, _____.

13. _____, ob er uns versteht.

14. _____, bis du das Glas Milch ausgetrunken hast.

Interrogatives

A **ja** or **nein** question begins with the verb, which is followed by the subject:

Ist Frau Gerber zu Hause?	*Is Ms. Gerber at home?*
Ja, sie ist zu Hause.	*Yes, she's at home.*
Nein, sie ist nicht zu Hause.	*No, she's not at home.*

It is possible to use such **ja** and **nein** questions as clauses with certain pat phrases, such as **wissen Sie** or **haben Sie gehört**. When this occurs, the conjunction **ob** can be required:

Hat er genug Geld?	*Does he have enough money?*
Ich weiß nicht, ob er genug Geld hat.	*I don't know if (whether) he has enough money.*
Wohnt sie noch in Amerika?	*Does she still live in America?*
Wir haben keine Ahnung, ob sie noch in Amerika wohnt.	*We have no idea if (whether) she still lives in America.*

But when a question begins with an interrogative word, that word can be used as a subordinating conjunction with the same pat phrases and **ob** is not needed. For example:

Wer steht an der Tür?	*Who is at the door?*
Ich weiß nicht, wer an der Tür steht.	*I don't know who is at the door.*
Wem gehört dieses Buch?	*Who(m) does this book belong to?*
Weiß jemand, wem dieses Buch gehört?	*Does anyone know to whom this book belongs?*
Um wie viel Uhr ist die Vorstellung?	*What time is the show?*
Bitte sagen Sie mir, um wie viel Uhr die Vorstellung ist.	*Please tell me what time the show is.*

Since these interrogative words are now functioning as subordinating conjunctions, they have the same effect on clauses as the other subordinating conjunctions. That is, the conjugated verb or auxiliary is the last element of the clause:

interrogative conjunction + verb
Er fragt, **wer** + das gesagt **hat**.
He asks who said that.

*Change the following questions to clauses preceded by **Ich weiß nicht**. Add **ob** where necessary.*

EXAMPLE: Ist der Bahnhof weit von hier?

Ich weiß nicht, ob der Bahnhof weit von hier ist.

1. Wer schwimmt in unserem Schwimmbad?

_____

2. Hat das Mädchen das Geld verloren?

_____

3. Warum drohte er dem alten Mann?

_____

4. Kann er diese Probleme lösen?

_____

5. Wie alt war sein Urgroßvater?

_____

6. Wem ist der Sohn ähnlich?

_____

7. Wonach fragte der kranke Herr?

_____

8. Wie lange wird die Vorstellung dauern?

_____

9. Was zeigt sie ihren Gästen?

_____

10. Entwickelte der Fotograf die Aufnahmen?

_____

11. Woran denkt die alte Dame gern?

_____

12. Um wen macht er sich viele Sorgen?

_____

13. Um wie viel Uhr geht der Mann in sein Büro?

_____

14. Was wird der Fremdenführer den Touristen zeigen wollen?

_____

Compose sentences using the words provided in each list. Add any necessary words.
Compose your tenses carefully.

EXAMPLE: wann / kommen / er / mit / sein / Freund / ?

Wann kam er mit seinem Freund?

1. Tina / bleiben / in / Stadt / bis / ihr / Tante / wieder / gesund / sein

_____

2. ich / erzählen / du / sein / Geschichte / damit / du / er / besser / verstehen

_____

3. während / es / donnern / blitzen / sitzen / wir / in / klein / Paddelboot

_____

4. Frau Benz / kaufen / Bluse / obwohl / Preis / sehr / hoch / sein

_____

5. Kind / sein / so / müde / dass / es / sofort / einschlafen

_____

6. seitdem / Wetter / wieder / schlecht / werden / müssen / Kinder / in / Keller / spielen

_____

7. wenn / sie / Verwandte / besuchen / sein / sie / am glücklichsten

_____

Write an original sentence with each of the following conjunctions.

1. ob

_____

2. weil

_____

3. damit

_____

4. als

_____

Relative pronouns

Relative pronouns are commonly used to combine two sentences that have the same noun or pronoun in both. One of them is changed to a relative pronoun, and the sentences are then combined:

> **identical noun + identical noun**
> *Do you know **the man**? + **The man** is a thief.*
> *Do you know the man, <u>who</u> is a thief?*

Two types of relative pronouns

In German, there are two basic types of relative pronouns. One is formed from the definite article, and the other is formed from the **der**-word **welcher**. Naturally, in German you have to consider the gender, number, and case when using relative pronouns. Let's look at their declension:

	MASCULINE	FEMININE	NEUTER	PLURAL
Definite article				
Nominative:	der	die	das	die
Accusative:	den	die	das	die
Dative:	dem	der	dem	denen
Possessive:	dessen	deren	dessen	deren
Welcher				
Nominative:	welcher	welche	welches	welche
Accusative:	welchen	welche	welches	welche
Dative:	welchem	welcher	welchem	welchen
Possessive:	dessen	deren	dessen	deren

Notice that both the definite article form and the **welcher** form have the identical possessive adjective where the genitive case would normally occur.

Just like English relative pronouns, German relative pronouns combine two sentences that have the same noun or pronoun in both. But in German, gender, number, and case must be considered. If the noun replaced by a relative pronoun is nominative, the relative pronoun must be nominative. For example:

Der Junge ist Amerikaner. Der Junge lernt Deutsch.	*The boy is an American. The boy is learning German.*
Der Junge, der Deutsch lernt, ist Amerikaner.	*The boy, who is learning German, is an American.*
Der Junge, welcher Deutsch lernt, ist Amerikaner.	⟶

51

Wo sind die Kinder? Die Kinder spielen Schach.	*Where are the children? The children are playing chess.*
Wo sind die Kinder, die Schach spielen?	*Where are the children who are playing chess?*
Wo sind die Kinder, welche Schach spielen?	⟶

main clause + der/die/das + relative clause with verb in final position

Das ist der Mann, + der + unser Haus kaufte.
That's the man who bought our house.

main clause + welcher + relative clause with verb in final position

Das ist der Mann, + welcher + unser Haus kaufte.
That's the man who bought our house.

If the noun replaced by a relative pronoun is accusative, the relative pronoun must be accusative. For example:

Sie ist die Frau. Thomas liebt die Frau.	*She is the woman. Thomas loves the woman.*
Sie ist die Frau, die Thomas liebt.	*She is the woman that Thomas loves.*
Sie ist die Frau, welche Thomas liebt.	
Er sprach mit dem Herrn. Niemand kennt den Herrn.	*He spoke with the gentleman. No one knows the gentleman.*
Er sprach mit dem Herrn, den niemand kennt.	*He spoke with the gentleman whom no one knows.*
Er sprach mit dem Herrn, welchen niemand kennt.	

If the noun replaced by a relative pronoun is dative, the relative pronoun must be dative. For example:

Kennst du die Leute? Er spricht mit den Leuten.	*Do you know the people? He is talking to the people.*
Kennst du die Leute, mit denen er spricht?	*Do you know the people that he is talking to?*
Kennst du die Leute, mit welchen er spricht?	
Die Dame ist eine Verwandte. Er hilft der Dame.	*The lady is a relative. He helps the lady.*
Die Dame, der er hilft, ist eine Verwandte.	*The lady that he helps is a relative.*
Die Dame, welcher er hilft, ist eine Verwandte.	

If the noun replaced by a relative pronoun is in the genitive case or is a possessive adjective, the relative pronoun must be in the possessive adjective form. For example:

Er sieht den Lehrer. Die Schüler des Lehrers singen ein Lied.	*He sees the teacher. The teacher's students are singing a song.*
Er sieht den Lehrer, dessen Schüler ein Lied singen.	*He sees the teacher, whose students are singing a song.*
Das ist die Richterin. Ihr Sohn wurde verhaftet.	*That's the judge. Her son was arrested.*
Das ist die Richterin, deren Sohn verhaftet wurde.	*That's the judge whose son was arrested.*

In the last example, the possessive adjective **ihr** refers to the noun **Richterin** and therefore is replaced by the corresponding feminine, singular relative pronoun.

It is probably wise to remind you that English has three types of relative pronouns: (1) *who* and *which,* which introduce a *non-restrictive* relative clause that gives parenthetical information; (2) *that,* which introduces a *restrictive* relative clause that helps to define the antecedent; and (3) an elliptical relative pronoun, which is understood but not spoken or written. All three types of English relative pronouns can be translated into German by the German definite article or **welcher.** For example:

Der Mann, den ich sah, ist ein Freund.
The man, whom I saw, is a friend.
The man that I saw is a friend.
The man I saw is a friend.

When the case of a German relative pronoun is determined by its accompanying preposition, the preposition precedes the relative pronoun. The position of a preposition in an English relative clause is more flexible. For example:

Das ist der Mann, für den er arbeitet.
That's the man for whom he works.
That's the man that he works for.
That's the man he works for.

Wo ist die Dame, mit der ich sprach?
Where's the woman with whom I spoke?
Where's the woman that I spoke with?
Where's the woman I spoke with?

Übung 7·1

Combine the following pairs of sentences by changing one of the identical nouns (or its corresponding possessive adjective) to the appropriate relative pronoun in its definite article form. Remember to take gender, number, and case into account.

EXAMPLE: Peter hat einen Wagen. Sie will den Wagen kaufen.

Peter hat einen Wagen, den sie kaufen will.

1. Die Frau wollte die Suppe nicht schmecken. Ihre Tochter ist Köchin.

   _____

2. Er hilft seinen Verwandten. Seine Verwandten wohnen in den Bergen.

   _____

3. Sie segelten zu einer Insel. Die Insel wurde von keinen Menschen bewohnt.

   _____

4. Es ist ein deutsches Flugzeug. Das Flugzeug ist eben gelandet.

   _____

5. Der alte Herr musste bei seinem Bruder wohnen. Sein Vermögen ging verloren.

   _____

6. Er trifft auf der Straße einen Freund. Das Gesicht seines Freundes ist ganz blass.

   _____

7. Sie sieht die Soldaten. Das kleine Dorf wurde von den Soldaten besetzt.

_____

8. Die Universität ist weltbekannt. In den Räumen der Universität findet eine Konferenz statt.

_____

9. Der Mann ist neulich gestorben. Tina hat für den Mann gearbeitet.

_____

10. Der Stuhl ist alt und wackelig. Oma sitzt auf dem Stuhl.

_____

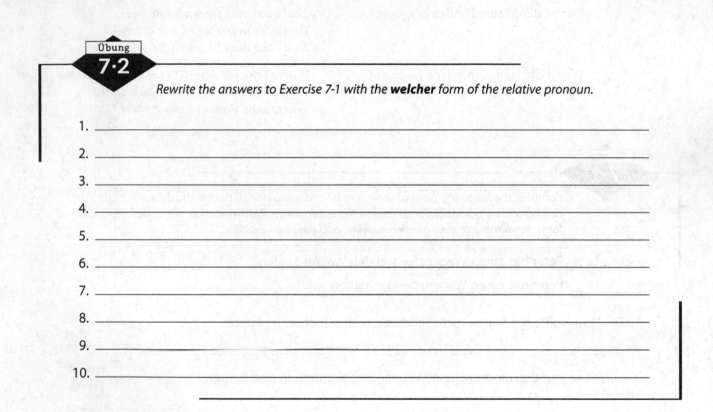

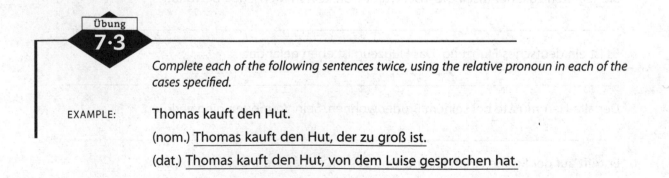

Übung

7·2

*Rewrite the answers to Exercise 7-1 with the **welcher** form of the relative pronoun.*

1. _____
2. _____
3. _____
4. _____
5. _____
6. _____
7. _____
8. _____
9. _____
10. _____

Übung

7·3

Complete each of the following sentences twice, using the relative pronoun in each of the cases specified.

EXAMPLE: Thomas kauft den Hut.

(nom.) <u>Thomas kauft den Hut, der zu groß ist.</u>

(dat.) <u>Thomas kauft den Hut, von dem Luise gesprochen hat.</u>

1. Er lud seine Freunde ein.

   a. (nom.) _____

   b. (acc.) _____

2. Wer hat die Uhr gekauft?

   a. (acc.) _____

   b. (dat.) _____

3. Andreas spielte mit dem Hund.

   a. (dat.) _____

   b. (poss.) _____

4. Alle respektieren die Richterin.

   a. (acc.) _____

   b. (dat.) _____

Wer and der

There is another aspect to relative pronouns. When no specific person is referred to in a sentence, the pronoun **wer** is used as a relative pronoun. It is usually paired with **der**, and the English meaning of this concept is *he, who*, or *who(so)ever*. For example:

> He who lies about me is no friend of mine.
> Whoever threw that snowball is in a lot of trouble.

Since German declines words like **wer** and **der**, this kind of relative pronoun usage can appear in all the cases:

Wer oft lügt, den respektiert niemand.	*He who often lies is respected by no one.*
Wen die Polizei verhaftet, dem kann man nicht helfen.	*No one can help him, whom the police arrest.*
Wem das imponiert, der ist wohl naiv.	*Whomever that impresses is probably naive.*
Wessen Brot man isst, dessen Lied man singt.	*If you eat his bread, you must dance to his tune.* (A saying)

You will notice that the declension of **wer** and **der** is dependent upon the use of each in its own clause.

Was

Something similar occurs with **was**. Use **was** if it refers to no specific object and can be translated as *that, which*, or *what(ever)*. For example:

Was billig ist, ist nicht immer gut.	*That which is cheap is not always good.*
Was sie sagte war Unsinn.	*What(ever) she said was nonsense.*

Was is also used as a relative pronoun after the demonstrative pronoun **das**. For example:

Sie verstand nichts von dem, was ich sagte.	*She didn't understand anything I said.*
Hast du das, was ich brauche?	*Do you have what I need?*

Was also becomes a relative pronoun after the following words: **alles**, **etwas**, **nichts**, **manches**, and **vieles**. For example:

Ist das alles, was Sie sagen wollen?	*Is that everything you want to say?*
Ich habe etwas, was dich freuen wird.	*I have something that will make you happy.*
Manches, was sie sagt, ist Unsinn.	*Some of what she says is nonsense.*
Rede nichts, was nicht alle hören dürfen.	*Say nothing that not everyone is allowed to hear.*
Es gibt vieles, was ich vergessen will.	*There's a lot that I want to forget.*

If an adjective is used as a noun, **was** acts as its relative pronoun:

Das ist das Schönste, was ich jemals gesehen habe.	*That's the nicest thing I've ever seen.*
Das war das Erste, was er sah.	*That was the first thing he saw.*

In addition, the relative pronoun **was** is used to introduce a relative clause when the antecedent is an entire clause. For example:

Onkel Karl reist heute ab, was ich sehr bedaure.	*Uncle Karl is leaving today, which I regret very much.*
Sie hat die Prüfung bestanden, was uns sehr erstaunte.	*She passed the test, which really surprised us.*

When a preposition is required with the relative pronoun **was**, the compound form **wo(r)** plus preposition is used. For example:

Hier gibt es nichts, wofür er sich interessiert.	*There's nothing here that interests him.*
Peter geht an die Universität, worauf sein Vater sehr stolz ist.	*Peter is going to college, which makes his father very proud.*

Übung
7·4

*Complete each sentence with an appropriate phrase that includes **wer** as the relative pronoun. Be careful to use the correct case of **wer**.*

EXAMPLE: <u>Wer mir in Not hilft</u>, der ist ein guter Freund.

1. _____, den kann sie nicht lieben.

2. _____, dem glaube ich nicht.

3. _____, der soll es nicht lesen.

4. _____, dem bleibt man fern.

5. _____, der ist gegen mich.

*Now complete each sentence with an appropriate conclusion beginning with a form of **der**.*

6. Wem es nicht gefällt, _____ .

7. Wer nicht gehorcht, _____ .

Übung

7·5

*Complete the following sentences with an appropriate antecedent for a **was** relative pronoun or an appropriate relative clause that is introduced by **was**.*

EXAMPLE: Das ist alles, was ich zu sagen habe.

1. Ist das das Beste, was _____ ?

2. Der Kranke hat etwas gegessen, was _____ .

3. Sie haben eine gute Prüfung gemacht, was _____ .

4. _____ , was billiger ist?

5. _____ , worum sich niemand kümmert.

6. _____ , was unvergesslich war.

7. Der Reisende erzählte vieles, was _____ .

8. _____ , worüber ich mich gar nicht freute.

9. Das war das Dümmste, was _____ .

Übung

7·6

This exercise contains a variety of relative pronoun types. Complete each sentence with an appropriate relative clause.

1. Er tanzt mit der Ausländerin, _____ .

2. Sie möchte alles wissen, _____ .

3. Der alte Hund ist gestorben, _____ .

4. Tue nichts, _____ !

5. Die Leute, _____ , fingen an zu schreien.

6. Hamburg ist eine Handelsstadt, _____ .

7. _____ , mit dem will ich nichts zu tun haben.

Write an original sentence that contains a relative clause. Use the word or phrase in parentheses as the relative pronoun.

1. (was)

_____

2. (mit denen)

_____

3. (dessen)

_____

4. (worüber)

_____

Extended modifiers

Modifiers include those words that help to describe a noun or pronoun. Some modifiers are called adjectives. If an adjective follows a verb like **sein** (*to be*) or **werden** (*to become*), it is a predicate adjective. For example:

Der Mann ist **alt**.	*The man is **old**.*
Sie wurde **krank**.	*She became **ill**.*

Attributive adjectives

If the adjective stands in front of the noun, it is called an attributive adjective and in German it will have an ending, and that ending will be determined by gender, number, and case. For example:

Kennst du den **alten** Mann?	*Do you know the **old** man?*
Sie besuchte ein **krankes** Kind.	*She visited a **sick** child.*

If you think about it, attributive adjectives play about the same role as certain relative clauses in which a predicate adjective is used. For example:

Kennst du den Mann, der alt ist?	*Do you know the man who is old?*
Kennst du den alten Mann?	*Do you know the old man?*
Sie besuchte ein Kind, das krank ist.	*She visited a child that is sick.*
Sie besuchte ein krankes Kind.	*She visited a sick child.*

The differences are the need for an ending on an attributive adjective and the need for a subject and verb in the relative clause. The use of an attributive adjective, therefore, is a bit more efficient and requires less time to say and less space to write.

Attributive adjectives can be extended somewhat by using other modifiers—adverbs—to define them. For example:

Sie hat einen ziemlich schnellen Wagen.	*She has a rather fast car.*
Das ist eine sehr wichtige Tatsache.	*That's a very important fact.*

The modifiers in the example sentences above were *extended* by the adverbs **ziemlich** and **sehr**. And, as you can clearly see, German and English function in the very same way when adverbs modify adjectives. By the way, that word *extended* will become important later on in this chapter.

Present participles

Present participles in German are formed quite simply. A -**d** ending is added to an infinitive. For example:

infinitive + d → present participle

störend	*disturbing*
entsprechend	*corresponding*
anregend	*stimulating*

Notice that the absence or presence of an inseparable or separable prefix does not affect the formation of present participles. Present participles are translated into English using an *-ing* suffix.

Present participles can be used as adverbs or adjectives, and when they are used as adjectives, they function as predicate or attributive adjectives. Let's look at some examples:

Sein Verhalten war sehr störend.	*His behavior was very disturbing.*
Er machte einen störenden Lärm.	*He made a disturbing noise.*
Sein letzter Roman war spannend.	*His last novel was thrilling.*
Das soll ein spannender Film sein.	*That's supposed to be a thrilling movie.*

Just like other modifiers, present participles can be modified by adverbs (**sehr störend**).

Übung 8·1

Form the present participle from the verb in each of the following phrases. Give the English translation of each participle.

EXAMPLE: ich laufe laufend *running*

1. du kommst an _____ _____

2. ich zwinge _____ _____

3. er belastet _____ _____

4. Sie stoßen ab _____ _____

5. du verhältst _____ _____

6. sie sieht an _____ _____

7. ihr fühlt mit _____ _____

Übung 8·2

Translate the following phrases into German. Provide the appropriate adjective ending for each present participle.

EXAMPLE: *the crying girl* das weinende Mädchen

1. *the sleeping children* _____

2. *the loudly barking dogs* _____

3. *from her disappointing answer*   _____

4. *a corresponding theory*   _____

5. *next to the laughing boy*   _____

6. *in the arriving train*   _____

7. *the slowly flowing water*   _____

Past participles

Past participles are used to form the perfect tenses. But just like present participles, they can also be used as adjectives:

> **(auxiliary omitted) + regular or irregular past participle → adjective**
>
> | | |
> |---|---|
> | (hat) gekocht | *cooked* |
> | (hat) versprochen | *promised* |
> | (ist) angekommen | *arrived* |

    Inseparable and separable prefixes affect the formation of a past participle. With inseparable prefixes, the past participle does not require an added **ge-** prefix, e.g., **besucht** (*visited*) and **vergangen** (*past*). With separable prefixes, the prefix is separated from the past participle by a **ge-** prefix (infix), placed between them, e.g., **mitgebracht** (*brought along*) and **zugenommen** (*increased*). Let's look at some example sentences that use past participles as predicate and attributive adjectives.

Er schien ganz gelassen.	*He seemed quite calm.*
Er hatte eine gelassene Reaktion.	*He had a calm reaction.*
Sie war gar nicht begeistert.	*She wasn't enthusiastic at all.*
Seine begeisterte Stimme war laut und schrill.	*His enthusiastic voice was loud and shrill.*

Übung

8·3

Translate the following phrases into German. Provide the appropriate adjective ending for each past participle.

EXAMPLE: *the written word*   das geschriebene Wort

1. *a broken man*   _____

2. *from the drunken man*   _____

3. *with the excited boys*   _____

4. *because of the poorly repaired motor*   _____

5. *a hard-boiled egg*   _____

6. *in the recently arrived train*   _____

7. *the United States*   _____

Extended modifiers

Just as attributive adjectives can replace a relative clause that contains a predicate adjective, so, too, can participles replace relative clauses. Look at the following example with adjectives:

das Haus, das klein ist	*the house that is small*
das kleine Haus	*the small house*

Compare that with the following examples, where participles replace the verbs in the relative clauses and the phrase that was previously expressed by the relative clause now precedes the noun that is modified:

das Haus, das an der Ecke steht	*the house that stands on the corner*
→ das an der Ecke stehende Haus	*the house that stands on the corner*
das Haus, das gestern zerstört wurde	*the house that was destroyed yesterday*
→ das gestern zerstörte Haus	*the house that was destroyed yesterday*

In both examples above the relative clause has been changed to an *extended modifier*, with the present or past participle acting as the modifier with the appropriate adjective ending. English does not use extended modifiers to the same degree as German, and German phrases that contain extended modifiers tend to be translated as relative clauses in English, as illustrated in the above examples.

der/die/das + participle + adjective ending
der + **sitzend** + **-e**
der vor der Tür sitzende Hund
the dog sitting in front of the door

Extended modifiers, especially those that are particularly long, tend to be used in formal writing or might be heard in a scholarly speech. When used in casual conversation, they sound cumbersome and lofty and are generally avoided.

If an active verb in a relative clause is changed into an extended modifier, a present participle is used: **der Mann, der singt = der singende Mann** (*the singing man*). If the verb is passive, a past participle is used: **das Lied, das gesungen wurde = das gesungene Lied** (*the song that was sung*). If the verb is a verb of motion or another verb that requires **sein** as its auxiliary, the tense of the participle is determined by the tense of the verb. For example:

der Zug, der gerade ankommt	*the train that is just now arriving*
der gerade ankommende Zug	*the train that is just now arriving*
der Zug, der schon angekommen ist	*the train that has already arrived*
der schon angekommene Zug	*the train that has already arrived*

If the verb is reflexive, the reflexive pronoun **sich** must be used with the participle:

der Mann, der sich schämt = der sich schämende Mann

Let's look at a sentence with an extended modifier formed from the past participle **bekannt**. Notice how it can grow with the addition of modifiers and prepositional phrases:

Er ist Politiker.	*He's a politician.*
Er ist ein bekannter Politiker.	*He's a well-known politician.*
Er ist ein sehr bekannter Politiker.	*He's a very well-known politician.*
Er ist ein in Europa sehr bekannter Politiker.	*He's a very well-known politician in Europe.*

Er ist ein bei Jugendlichen in Europa sehr bekannter Politiker.	*He's a very well-known politician among young people in Europe.*

The English translation of this final sentence could contain a relative clause:

He's a politician who is very well-known among young people in Europe.

**Übung
8·4**

Rewrite the following sentences by changing the verb phrase in each relative clause into an extended modifier.

EXAMPLE: Die Frau, die im Wohnzimmer sitzt, ist meine Schwester.

Die im Wohnzimmer sitzende Frau ist meine Schwester.

1. Der Polizist, der den Rechtsanwalt anruft, ist in Not.

_____

2. Ich hasse das Wetter, das sich so schnell verändert.

_____

3. Sein Gewinn, der uns überrascht, erfreute seine Frau.

_____

4. Niemand will dem Taschendieb helfen, der zum vierten Mal verhaftet worden ist.

_____

5. Die langen Kerzen, die so trüb brennen, standen auf dem Klavier.

_____

6. Das ist der Professor, der von seinen ehemaligen Studenten besucht wurde.

_____

7. Sie ist sehr stolz auf die Studentinnen, die konzentriert arbeiten.

_____

8. Der Kranke, der an seinen Wunden stirbt, hat keine Familie.

_____

9. Kannten Sie die Frau, die gestern Abend verstorben ist?

_____

10. Der Soldat, der sich so langsam bewegte, war verwundet.

_____

Rewrite the following sentences by adding a modifier or prepositional phrase to the extended modifier.

EXAMPLE: Er nimmt das Problem mit geöffneten Augen an.

Er nimmt das Problem mit weit geöffneten Augen an.

1. Sie bekam einen gut geschriebenen Brief.

    _____

2. Er wollte die längst aufgegessene Torte probieren.

    _____

3. Das verkaufte Auto muss schon repariert werden.

    _____

4. Ausgebildete Menschen werden von unserer Firma gesucht.

    _____

5. Die Eltern suchten nach ihrem verschwundenen Sohn.

    _____

6. Der geschiedene Mann will eine jüngere Frau heiraten.

    _____

7. Das spielende Kind fing an zu weinen.

    _____

Combine each list of words into an extended modifier for the noun given.

EXAMPLE: schön / singen / Vogel

der schön singende Vogel

1. auf / Herd / stehen / Suppe

    _____

2. von / Armee / zerstören / Dorf

    _____

3. vor / Angst / zittern / Kätzchen

    _____

4. laut / reden / Prediger

_____

5. vor / zwei / Jahr / bauen / Häuser

_____

6. brennen / neulich / verkaufen / Haus

_____

7. aus / zehn / Amerikaner / bestehen / Reisegruppe

_____

Übung
8·7

Write original sentences that include an extended modifier formed from the relative clause provided. **DER** _represents the definite article_ **der**, **die**, _or_ **das**. _The gender and case of the articles you use will change depending upon the context._

EXAMPLE: DER das Museum besucht

             Wir begegneten den das Museum besuchenden Touristen.

1. DER von dem Studenten getrunken wurde

_____

2. DER von der Köchin gebacken worden ist

_____

3. DER sich die Haare kämmt

_____

4. DER auf dem Boden eingeschlafen ist

_____

Adjectives

Adjectives are very useful in making sentences more interesting or for providing clarity. They modify nouns and pronouns and can be predicative or attributive:

Predicative:	*He is **lucky**.*
Attributive:	*John is a **lucky** guy.*

Adjectives work the same way in German, with the exception of requiring an ending when used attributively:

- Predicative:

    subject + linking verb + adjective
    Die Frau + ist + krank.
    The woman is sick.

- Attributive:

    subject + verb + declined adjective + object
    Die Frau + hilft + dem kranken + Kind.
    The woman helps the sick child.

The pattern illustrated above shows a declined adjective in the dative case. However, declined adjectives occur in all cases (nominative, accusative, dative, and genitive).

Predicative:	Sie ist klug.	*She is smart.*
Attributive:	Tina ist eine kluge Frau.	*Tina is a smart woman.*

When an adjective ending is required, the nominative singular of all three genders and the accusative singular of the feminine and neuter indicate gender differently, depending upon whether the determiner used is a **der**-word or an **ein**-word:

DER-WORDS		**EIN**-WORDS	
der, die, das	*the*	ein, eine	*a, an, one*
dieser	*this*	mein	*my*
jener	*that*	dein	*your*
jeder	*each*	sein	*his*
mancher	*many a*	ihr	*her, their*
solcher	*such*	unser	*our*
welcher	*which, what*	euer	*your*
derjenige	*the one*	Ihr	*your*
derselbe	*the same*	kein	*not any*

With **der**-words, gender is shown in the determiner. With **ein**-words, gender is shown in the adjective. For example:

Nominative:	der alte Mann	diese alte Frau	jedes alte Haus
Accusative:	*	diese alte Frau	jedes alte Haus
	the old man	*this old woman*	*each old house*
Nominative:	ein alter Mann	seine alte Frau	kein altes Haus
Accusative:	*	seine alte Frau	kein altes Haus
	an old man	*his old wife*	*no old house*

*(We'll look at the masculine accusative forms later.)

With both kinds of determiners, the adjective ending is always **-en** in the masculine accusative and throughout the dative and genitive with feminine and neuter nouns. In the plural, all adjectives with these determiners have an **-en** ending. For example:

Singular

Accusative:	jenen guten Mann	*	*
Dative:	jenem guten Mann	einer klugen Frau	welchem neuen Haus
Genitive:	jenes guten Mannes	einer klugen Frau	welches neuen Hauses
	that good man	*a smart woman*	*which new house*

*(See above for feminine and neuter accusative forms.)

Plural

Nominative:	seine alten Bücher
Accusative:	seine alten Bücher
Dative:	seinen alten Büchern
Genitive:	seiner alten Bücher
	his old books

The determiners **alle** (*all*) and **beide** (*both*) are exceptions. They are **der**-words but are only used in the plural. For example:

Nominative:	alle alten Bücher	beide guten Kinder
Accusative:	alle alten Bücher	beide guten Kinder
Dative:	allen alten Büchern	beiden guten Kindern
Genitive:	aller alten Bücher	beider guten Kinder
	all old books	*both good children*

Übung

9·1

Provide an appropriate adjective for each of the following phrases. Then use that phrase in a sentence in the same case in which it is given.

EXAMPLE: mit dem _____ Kind

mit dem <u>kranken</u> Kind

<u>Sie wollte mit dem kranken Kind sprechen.</u>

1. a. von seiner _____ Mutter

   b. _____

2. a. ein _____ Gebäude

   b. _____

3. a. durch einen _____ Tunnel

   b. _____

4. a. jenes _____ Professors

   b. _____

5. a. für unsere _____ Verwandten

   b. _____

6. a. alle _____ Reisenden

   b. _____

7. a. beiden _____ Jungen

   b. _____

8. a. trotz des _____ Wetters

   b. _____

9. a. während einer _____ Oper

   b. _____

10. a. gegen Ihren _____ Chef

    b. _____

Unpreceded adjectives

There are times when a determiner does not precede an adjective. In such cases, the adjective will
have the ending that would normally have been on an **ein**-word. This is true in both the singular
and plural. Examples of *unpreceded adjectives*:

Nominative:	kalter Kaffee	kalte Suppe	kaltes Eis	kalte Finger
Accusative:	kalten Kaffee	kalte Suppe	kaltes Eis	kalte Finger
Dative:	kaltem Kaffee	kalter Suppe	kaltem Eis	kalten Fingern
Genitive:	kalten Kaffees	kalter Suppe	kalten Eises	kalter Finger
	cold coffee	*cold soup*	*cold ice*	*cold fingers*

Übung
9·2

Fill in the blanks in each sentence with an appropriate adjective or determiner.

1. Dieser _____ Mann trinkt nur _____ Tee.

2. _____ Bücher kosten mehr als diese _____ Hefte.

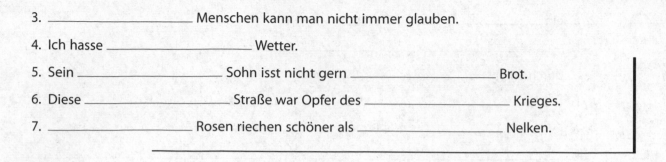

3. _____ Menschen kann man nicht immer glauben.

4. Ich hasse _____ Wetter.

5. Sein _____ Sohn isst nicht gern _____ Brot.

6. Diese _____ Straße war Opfer des _____ Krieges.

7. _____ Rosen riechen schöner als _____ Nelken.

Mancher, solcher, welcher

Special mention must be made of three of the **der**-words: **mancher**, **solcher**, **welcher**. They can be used in two ways: (1) just like other **der**-words; and (2) in an undeclined form that requires the adjective that follows it to use the endings that are required with unpreceded adjectives. For example:

Nominative:	mancher gute Mann	manch guter Mann
Accusative:	manchen guten Mann	manch guten Mann
Dative:	manchem guten Mann	manch gutem Mann
Genitive:	manches guten Mannes	manch guten Mannes
	many a good man	*many a good man*

Nominative:	welches neue Auto	welch schöner Augenblick
Accusative:	welches neue Auto	welch schönen Augenblick
Dative:	welchem neuen Auto	welch schönem Augenblick
Genitive:	welches neuen Autos	welch schönen Augenblicks
	which new car	*what a beautiful moment*

However, **solcher** as a **der**-word tends to be used in the plural, and in the singular it follows **ein** and is declined like an adjective:

Nominative:	solche alten Leute	eine solche Bluse
Accusative:	solche alten Leute	eine solche Bluse
Dative:	solchen alten Leuten	einer solchen Bluse
Genitive:	solcher alten Leute	einer solchen Bluse
	such old people	*such a blouse*

Just like the usage of **manch**, **solch**, and **welch** illustrated above, there are other occasions when an adjective requires the same endings as in the previous examples. They occur with **etwas**, **mehr**, **viel**, **wenig**, and with numbers, and can be used in both singular and plural phrases. For example:

etwas schwarzer Marmor	*some black marble*
mehr interessante Bücher	*more interesting books*
viel amerikanisches Geld	*much American money*
wenig heiße Tage	*few hot days*

The declension for such phrases follows the pattern illustrated by **manch guter Mann**, above.

Compose original phrases in the nominative case singular with the cue words provided.

EXAMPLE: manch   manch junger Mann

1. manch _____
2. welch _____
3. etwas _____
4. mehr _____
5. wenig _____

Now rewrite each phrase in the dative case with an appropriate dative preposition.

EXAMPLE: mit manch jungem Mann

6. _____
7. _____
8. _____
9. _____
10. _____

Plural-only determiners

Certain determiners are used only in the plural. They identify quantities, and like the numbers cause adjectives to be declined like unpreceded adjectives. These determiners are **einige**, **mehrere**, **viele**, and **wenige**. You will notice that **viele** and **wenige**, although used in the same way as **viel** and **wenig**, decline, but the adjectives that follow **viele** and **wenige** still require the same endings as unpreceded adjectives. Some examples:

Nominative:	einige gute Kinder	viele neue Schulen
Accusative:	einige gute Kinder	viele neue Schulen
Dative:	einigen guten Kindern	vielen neuen Schulen
Genitive:	einiger guter Kinder	vieler neuer Schulen
	some good children	*many new schools*
Nominative:	mehrere gute Kinder	wenige neue Schulen
Accusative:	mehrere gute Kinder	wenige neue Schulen
Dative:	mehreren guten Kindern	wenigen neuen Schulen
Genitive:	mehrerer guter Kinder	weniger neuer Schulen
	several good children	*few new schools*

Compose original phrases in the nominative case plural with the cue words provided.

EXAMPLE: viele   viele junge Leute

1. vier   _____

2. einige   _____

3. alle   _____

4. mehrere   _____

5. beide   _____

Now rewrite each phrase in the genitive case.

EXAMPLE: vieler junger Leute

6. _____

7. _____

8. _____

9. _____

10. _____

Comparative and superlative

When comparing two people or things, the comparative form of an adjective is used. In general, a comparative is formed by adding **-er** to the adjective:

POSITIVE		COMPARATIVE	
laut	*loud*	lauter	*louder*
schnell	*fast*	schneller	*faster*
interessant	*interesting*	interessanter	*more interesting*

The conjunction **als** (*than*) can be added to make the comparison:

Dieser Wagen ist schneller als jener.   *This car is faster than that one.*

Superlatives used as predicate adjectives are formed by preceding them with the prepositional phrase **am (an dem)** and adding the suffix **-sten**:

POSITIVE		SUPERLATIVE	
laut	*loud*	am lautesten	*the loudest*
schnell	*fast*	am schnellsten	*the fastest*
interessant	*interesting*	am interessantesten	*the most interesting*

Many adjectives that have an **a**, **o**, or **u** (called umlaut vowels) in their base form will require an umlaut in the comparative and superlative:

POSITIVE		COMPARATIVE		SUPERLATIVE	
alt	*old*	älter	*older*	am ältesten	*the oldest*
groß	*big*	größer	*bigger*	am größten	*the biggest*
jung	*young*	jünger	*younger*	am jüngsten	*the youngest*

When an adjective or adverb ends in **-d**, **-t**, **-s**, **-ss**, **-ß**, or **-z**, the superlative suffix will be **-esten**. For example:

am ältesten	*the oldest*
am blödesten	*the most idiotic*
am kürzesten	*the shortest*

Just as English has a few irregular forms in the comparative and superlative, so, too, does German.

POSITIVE		COMPARATIVE		SUPERLATIVE	
bald	*soon*	eher	*soonest*	am ehesten	*the soonest*
groß	*big*	größer	*bigger*	am größten	*the biggest*
gut	*good*	besser	*better*	am besten	*the best*
hoch	*high*	höher	*higher*	am höchsten	*the highest*
nah	*near*	näher	*nearer*	am nächsten	*the nearest*

Another spelling concern arises with adjectives that end in **-el**, **-en**, and **-er**. In the comparative the **-e-** is usually dropped:

dunkel	*dark*	dunkler	*darker*
trocken	*dry*	trockner	*drier*
teuer	*expensive*	teurer	*more expensive*

Comparatives and superlatives can be used in the same way as predicate adjectives:

Dieses Radio ist lauter als jenes.	*This radio is louder than that one.*
Euer Radio ist am lautesten.	*Your radio is the loudest.*

When a comparative or superlative adjective is used attributively, it requires the same kinds of endings as other adjectives:

Nominative:	dieser längere Satz	*this longer sentence*
Accusative:	die kürzesten Briefe	*the shortest letters*
Dative:	einem größeren Problem	*a bigger problem*
Genitive:	seiner besten Werke	*his best works*

Using the adjective and the three noun phrases provided in each item, form sentences with a positive, a comparative, and a superlative adjective.

EXAMPLE: nett / der Lehrer / die Lehrerin / der neue Studienrat

Der Lehrer ist nett.

Die Lehrerin ist netter als der Lehrer.

Der neue Studienrat ist am nettesten.

1. klein / der braune Hund / der schwarze Hund / die weiße Katze

   a. _____

   b. _____

   c. _____

2. gut / sein neuer Roman / sein letzter Roman / seine Gedichte

   a. _____

   b. _____

   c. _____

3. hell / diese weiße Kerze / jene Laterne / die neue Stehlampe

   a. _____

   b. _____

   c. _____

Adjectives as nouns

Just about any adjective can be used as a noun in German. And when it is, it is capitalized, but it still functions as an adjective; that is, it still shows the appropriate number, gender, and case by its ending. For example:

Welcher Mann ist krank?	*Which man is sick?*
Der Alte.	*The old (one, man).*
Mit welcher Frau sprach er?	*What woman did he speak with?*
Mit der Schönen.	*With the pretty (one, woman).*

Here are some adjectives and participles that commonly function as nouns:

der Angestellte	*employee*
der Bekannte	*acquaintance*
der Deutsche	*German*
der Erwachsene	*adult*
der Fremde	*stranger*
der Jugendliche	*youth*
der Junge	*boy*

der Reisende	*traveler*
der Verletzte	*injured party*
der Verwandte	*relative*

Naturally, most nouns given above could be feminine or plural.

When adjectives are used as neuter nouns, they often express abstract ideas. For example:

| Sie will das Beste, was Sie haben. | *She wants the best one you have.* |
| Ich habe nichts Neues gehört. | *I haven't heard anything new.* |

Compose sentences using the words provided in each list. Add any necessary words.

EXAMPLE: morgen / kommen / er / mit / neu /Freund

Morgen kommt er mit einem neuen Freund.

1. bei / solch / schön / Wetter / gehen / jung / Ehepaar / oft / spazieren

_____

2. ein / jung / Dame / wollen / warm / Mantel / kaufen

_____

3. der / alt / sich erinnern / an / froh / Tage / sein / Jugend

_____

4. dies / Schmetterlinge / lieben / farbig / duftend / Rosen

_____

Adverbs

Adverbial expressions appear as single words or in the form of phrases. In either case, their function is the same: to explain how, when, where, or why about an action or event. Below is a list of some commonly used single-word adverbs:

neulich	*recently*
niemals	*never*
oft	*often*
telefonisch	*by telephone*
wahrscheinlich	*probably*

And the following are adverbs that appear in phrase form:

am schnellsten	*the fastest*
das ganze Jahr	*the whole year*
im Winter	*in the winter*
mit dem Zug	*by train*
vor einer Woche	*a week ago*

With the exception of the phrase **das ganze Jahr**, each of the examples in the above list is a prepositional phrase. A large number of adverbial phrases are, indeed, prepositional phrases.

Like **das ganze Jahr**, many adverbial expressions that tell *when* something occurs are given in the accusative case. For example:

| Ich war **den ganzen Tag** in Bremen. | *I was in Bremen **all day**.* |
| Onkel Peter kommt **nächste Woche**. | *Uncle Peter is coming **next week**.* |

Adverbs of Degree

The function of adverbs is not as simple as *modifying a verb, an adverb,* or *an adjective,* because adverbs modify in a variety of ways. Some merely qualify the *degree* of an adverb or adjective used in a sentence. For example:

außerordentlich	*exceptionally*	relativ	*relatively*
etwas	*somewhat*	sehr	*very*
fast	*almost*	total	*totally*
ganz	*quite*	völlig	*completely*
gewöhnlich	*usually*	wenig	*little*
nur	*only*	ziemlich	*rather*
recht	*quite, rather*	zu	*too*

Consider the meaning of the preceding adverbs. They generally would not stand alone but would be used to modify another word. Let's look at some example sentences:

Die Studentin muss sehr fleißig arbeiten.	*The student has to work very diligently.*
Seine Rede war außerordentlich langweilig.	*His speech was exceptionally boring.*
Wir hatten in diesem Jahr einen relativ warmen Winter.	*We had a relatively warm winter this year.*

verb + adverb	Er singt gut.
adverb + adverb	Er singt sehr gut.
adverb + adjective	Es ist ein ziemlich altes Haus.

Übung
10·1

Rewrite each sentence twice, using each of the two adverbs provided in parentheses, in turn.

EXAMPLE: Er kommt spät.

a. (sehr) <u>Er kommt sehr spät.</u>

b. (zu) <u>Er kommt zu spät.</u>

1. Meine Schwester spielt gut Geige.

a. (ziemlich) _____

b. (recht) _____

2. Bach war schon als Kind musikalisch.

a. (außerordentlich) _____

b. (sehr) _____

Follow the same directions but provide your own adverbs. Use those already given or any others that are appropriate for the sentences.

3. Meine Tante ist vierzig Jahre alt.

a. _____

b. _____

4. Der faule Student ist durchgefallen.

a. _____

b. _____

Modal adverbs

Some adverbs portray an attitude toward a statement or are part of the answer to a yes or no question. Germans call such adverbs **modale Adverbien** (*modal adverbs*). They comment on some occurrence or show a point of view. Some commonly used adverbs of this type are:

auf jeden Fall	*in any case*	selbstverständlich	*naturally*
bestimmt	*definitely*	sicher	*surely, safely*
gewiss	*certainly*	tatsächlich	*actually, really*
hoffentlich	*hopefully*	unbedingt	*absolutely*
leider	*unfortunately*	wahrscheinlich	*probably*
natürlich	*naturally*	wirklich	*really*
ohne Zweifel	*without a doubt*		

Such adverbs are often used in an elliptical phrase, meaning that they can stand alone, because the content of the response is understood. For example:

—Kann Erik uns helfen?	—*Can Erik help us?*
—Selbstverständlich.	—*Naturally.*
—Haben sie genug Geld, um ins Kino zu gehen?	—*Do they have enough money to go to the movies?*
—Hoffentlich.	—*Hopefully. (I hope so.)*
—Ist deine Mutter wieder gesund?	—*Is your mother well again?*
—Leider nicht.	—*Unfortunately, not.*

In addition, adverbs of this type are used in complete sentences like other adverbs:

Es ist wirklich kalt geworden.	*It's gotten really cold.*
Der Kranke wird wahrscheinlich heute abend sterben.	*The patient will probably die this evening.*

Übung
10·2

Compose sentences using the words provided in each list. Add any necessary words.

EXAMPLE: er / kaufen / ziemlich / teuer / Anzug

Er kauft einen ziemlich teuren Anzug.

1. ihr / jüngste / Sohn / sein / wirklich / faul

_____

2. es / geben / heute / bestimmt / noch / Regen

_____

3. klein / Hündchen / sein / sehr / schwach / und / sein / leider / sterben

_____

4. Karl / werden / wir / wahrscheinlich / zu / Bahnhof / begleiten

_____

Adverbs and word order

Three major categories of adverbs are those that show *time*, *manner*, and *place*. They can be single words or phrases and are found in abundance in the language. Some examples:

TIME		MANNER	
damals	*then*	anders	*differently*
gestern	*yesterday*	dadurch	*through it, as a result*
heute	*today*	irgendwie	*somehow*
im Sommer	*in summer*	langsam	*slowly*
lange	*long*	mit dem Bus	*by bus*
manchmal	*sometimes*	mit Müh und Not	*with great difficulty*
morgen	*tomorrow*	schnell	*fast*
nächste Woche	*next week*	sorglos	*carelessly*
oft	*often*	telefonisch	*by telephone*
selten	*seldom*	vorsichtig	*carefully*

PLACE	
da, dort	*there*
hier	*here*
hinten	*behind, in the back*
in Hamburg	*in Hamburg*
nach Hause	*home(ward)*
nirgendwo	*nowhere*
oben	*above, overhead*
überall	*everywhere*
unterwegs	*on the way*
zu Hause	*at home*

Adverbs of place can describe location at a place or motion to a place. For example:

Location:	Er wohnt hier.	*He lives here.*
Motion:	Er kommt hierher.	*He comes here.*
Location:	Sie bleibt zu Hause.	*She remains at home.*
Motion:	Sie muss nach Hause gehen.	*She has to go home.*
Location:	Ich arbeite in der Stadt.	*I work in the city.*
Motion:	Ich fahre in die Stadt.	*I drive to the city.*

Adverbs cannot be placed in a German sentence at random. Adverbs that describe place appear last in a sentence. Adverbs of manner precede them. Adverbs of time precede adverbs of manner. And if an adverb that describes a point of view is in a sentence, it will precede all the others. For example:

Place:	Tina wird nach Bonn fahren.	*Tina will go to Bonn.*
Manner:	Tina wird mit dem Auto nach Bonn fahren.	*Tina will go to Bonn by car.*
Time:	Tina wird am Freitag mit dem Auto nach Bonn fahren.	*Tina will go to Bonn by car on Friday.*
Point of view:	Tina wird leider am Freitag mit dem Auto nach Bonn fahren.	*Unfortunately, Tina will go to Bonn by car on Friday.*

The position of adverbs in a sentence is generally:

point of view + time + manner + place

Fill in the blanks in each sentence with an adverbial expression from the following list.

auswendig (*by heart*)	plötzlich (*suddenly*)
endlich (*finally*)	schriftlich (*in writing*)
ganz (*quite*)	täglich (*daily*)
immer (*always*)	ungefähr (*approximately*)
natürlich (*naturally*)	vielleicht (*perhaps*)
niemals (*never*)	wochenlang (*for weeks*)

EXAMPLE: Es ist _____ wieder warm geworden.

Es ist <u>endlich</u> wieder warm geworden.

1. Das ist mir _____ egal.

2. Ich kann den alten Mann nicht _____ verstehen.

3. _____ hat jemand diesen Regenschirm vergessen.

4. Ich bin _____ in Europa gewesen aber möchte gern dorthin reisen.

5. Die alte Frau geht _____ ins Kino.

6. _____ sah er seinen größten Feind um die Ecke kommen.

7. Ihr müsst das lange Gedicht _____ lernen.

8. Bist du _____ damit fertig?

9. Warum lügst du _____ ?

10. _____ kann ich Ihnen damit helfen.

Adverbs in the comparative and superlative

Just like adjectives, adverbs have comparative and superlative forms. Unlike adjectives, however, adverbs do not require various endings that reflect gender, case, and number. Their only declensional form appears in the superlative, with the preposition **am (an dem)**. Let's look at some examples:

POSITIVE		COMPARATIVE		SUPERLATIVE	
gut	*good, well*	besser	*better*	am besten	*best*
schnell	*fast*	schneller	*faster*	am schnellsten	*fastest*
langsam	*slowly*	langsamer	*slower*	am langsamsten	*slowest*
schlecht	*badly*	schlechter	*worse*	am schlechtesten	*worst*

Rewrite each sentence twice, changing the adverb in the positive to an adverb in the comparative and then in the superlative.

EXAMPLE: Er läuft schnell.

        a. <u>Er läuft schneller.</u>

        b. <u>Er läuft am schnellsten.</u>

1. Der jüngere Bariton singt schön.

    a. _____

    b. _____

2. Diese Jungen haben sich schlecht benommen.

    a. _____

    b. _____

3. Mein Onkel wohnt weit von hier.

    a. _____

    b. _____

4. Sein Vortrag dauerte lang.

    a. _____

    b. _____

Write original sentences using the adverbs provided.

EXAMPLE: sehr <u>Diese Erzählung ist sehr interessant.</u>

1. wahrscheinlich _____

2. immer _____

3. nächsten Freitag _____

4. spät _____

5. im Herbst _____

6. vor der Tür _____

7. ziemlich _____

Pronouns

Pronouns are words that stand in place of a noun. In German, third person pronouns must be true to the gender, number, and case of the nouns they replace:

> der Mann → *masculine singular nominative* → er
> die Frau → *feminine singular dative* → ihr
> das Kind → *neuter singular accusative* → es
> die Kinder → *plural nominative* → sie

First, let's look at all the personal pronouns in the three cases and as possessive adjectives:

NOM.	ACC.	DAT.	POSS.	
ich	mich	mir	mein	*I, me, my*
du	dich	dir	dein	*you, your* (*informal singular*)
er	ihn	ihm	sein	*he/it, his/its*
sie	sie	ihr	ihr	*she/it, her/its*
es	es	ihm	sein	*it, its*
wir	uns	uns	unser	*we, us, our*
ihr	euch	euch	euer	*you, your* (*informal plural*)
Sie	Sie	Ihnen	Ihr	*you, your* (*formal singular or plural*)
sie	sie	ihnen	ihr	*they, them, their*

Most German personal pronouns are used like their English counterparts. But the third person pronouns (**er, sie, es**) reflect the gender of the word they replace: masculine, feminine, or neuter—whether animate or inanimate. The English meaning of the noun should not be considered, because sexual gender does not determine the gender of a German pronoun. For example:

MASCULINE		PRONOUN	
der Lehrer	*teacher*	er	*he*
der Garten	*garden*	er	*it*

FEMININE		PRONOUN	
die Richterin	*judge*	sie	*she*
die Blume	*flower*	sie	*it*

NEUTER		PRONOUN	
das Kind	*child*	es	*he, she*
das Dorf	*village*	es	*it*

In the plural, the German and English third person pronouns are used identically: gender is not considered, and all nouns are replaced by a single pronoun, **sie** (*they*):

PLURAL		PRONOUN	
die Leute	*people*	sie	*they*
die Zeitungen	*newspapers*	sie	*they*

Man

The third person pronoun **man** is generally translated as *one*. But in reality it has other English translations: *you, they, someone, people,* and certain phrases expressed in the passive voice. For example, the most common use of **man** is in sentences such as these:

Man soll nicht fluchen.	**One** *should not curse.*
Man kann nie wissen.	**You** *can never tell.*
Man hat ihn dafür verprügelt.	**They** *beat him up for it.*

But other translations can also be used for this pronoun:

Man wartet vor dem Eingang.	*Someone is waiting in front of the entrance.*
Damals glaubte man, dass die Erde flach war.	*Back then people believed the earth was flat.*
Man hat herausgefunden, dass sie das Geld gestohlen hat.	*It was discovered that she stole the money.*

The pronoun **man** is not a substitute for a specific noun. It is used to express what people do in general or to point out that the person or persons carrying out an action are unknown. **Man** is used only as a replacement for people and is only used in the nominative case. If another case is required, a form of **einer** is used:

Man ist froh, wenn **einem** ein kleines Geschenk gegeben wird.	*One is happy when one is given a little gift.*

When forming German sentences, it is wise to consider carefully whether the English relates to people in general or specific people. This will help to determine whether **man** is the appropriate pronoun for a sentence. For example:

Man liebte den alten König.	*People loved the old king.* (*general*)
Das Volk des Dorfes liebte den alten König.	*The people of the village loved the old king.* (*specific*)

◆ Übung
11·1

*Rewrite each sentence, changing the underlined words and phrases to **man** or **einer**, as appropriate. Make any other necessary changes.*

EXAMPLE: Die Jungen sollen nicht fluchen.

Man soll nicht fluchen.

1. Die Politiker erwarten von den Bürgern respektiert zu werden.

2. Oft tut der Mann, was er nicht tun soll.

_____

3. Die Firma soll ihnen mehr Lohn geben.

_____

4. Den Kindern soll so viel wie möglich geholfen werden.

_____

5. Es wird oft gesagt, dass sie miteinander nie auskommen werden.

_____

6. Die Frauen müssen ihn lange kennen, bis sie ihn verstehen.

_____

7. Ein Fremder stand am Fenster und klopfte.

_____

Jemand and niemand

The third person pronouns **jemand** and **niemand** refer to *someone* and *no one*. Specific people are not identified. Unlike **man**, these two pronouns can be declined, although the accusative and dative endings are optional:

Nominative:	niemand	jemand
Accusative:	niemand(en)	jemand(en)
Dative:	niemand(em)	jemand(em)
Genitive:	niemandes	jemandes

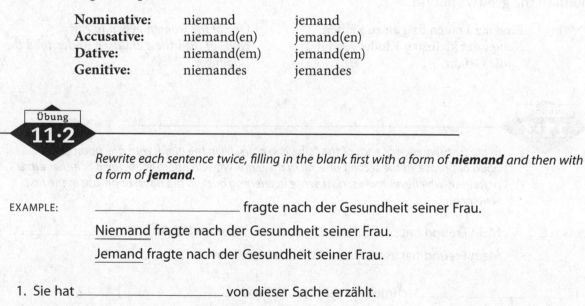

Übung
11·2

*Rewrite each sentence twice, filling in the blank first with a form of **niemand** and then with a form of **jemand**.*

EXAMPLE: _____ fragte nach der Gesundheit seiner Frau.

Niemand fragte nach der Gesundheit seiner Frau.

Jemand fragte nach der Gesundheit seiner Frau.

1. Sie hat _____ von dieser Sache erzählt.

a. _____

b. _____

2. Ich kannte _____ auf der Geburtstagsfeier.

a. _____

b. _____

3. _____ wollte das alte Haus kaufen.

   a. _____

   b. _____

4. Du musst doch _____ glauben.

   a. _____

   b. _____

Einer and keiner

The pronouns **einer** and **keiner** are similar to **niemand** and **jemand** in usage. They refer to *some-one* or *no one/none* and are declined like **ein**-words. However, they also reflect gender and, in the case of **keiner**, can occur in the plural. Let's look at the declension of **keiner**:

	MASC.	FEM.	NEUT.	PL.
Nominative:	keiner	keine	keines	keine
Accusative:	keinen	keine	keines	keine
Dative:	keinem	keiner	keinem	keinen
Genitive:	keines	keiner	keines	keiner

When forming sentences, remember that a genitive phrase can follow **einer** (*one of . . .*) or **keiner** (*none of . . .*). The gender ending of **einer** or **keiner** is determined by the gender of the noun in the genitive phrase:

Eine der Frauen fing an zu weinen.	*One of the women began to cry.*
Keines der kleinsten Kinder verstand die Gefahr.	*None of the littlest children understood the danger.*

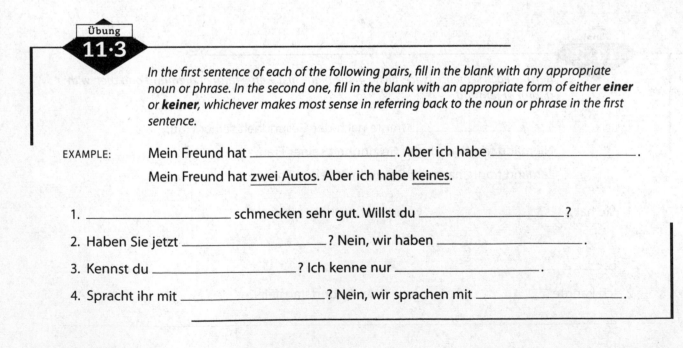

Übung
11·3

*In the first sentence of each of the following pairs, fill in the blank with any appropriate noun or phrase. In the second one, fill in the blank with an appropriate form of either **einer** or **keiner**, whichever makes most sense in referring back to the noun or phrase in the first sentence.*

EXAMPLE: Mein Freund hat _____. Aber ich habe _____.

Mein Freund hat <u>zwei Autos</u>. Aber ich habe <u>keines</u>.

1. _____ schmecken sehr gut. Willst du _____?

2. Haben Sie jetzt _____? Nein, wir haben _____.

3. Kennst du _____? Ich kenne nur _____.

4. Spracht ihr mit _____? Nein, wir sprachen mit _____.

Einander

The reciprocal pronoun **einander** (*one another, each other*) refers to an action that is shared by two parties. It is used in the form **einander** or combined with a preposition, such as **miteinander** (*with one another, with each other*). When **einander** is combined with a preposition, the preposition becomes a prefix and the two parts are written as one word.

When two parties carry out the same action in two different sentences, the sentences can be combined as one with a form of **einander**. For example:

Tina liebt Erik. Erik liebt Tina.	*Tina loves Erik. Erik loves Tina.*
→ Tina und Erik lieben einander.	*Tina and Erik love one another.*
Er spricht mit ihr. Sie spricht mit ihm.	*He speaks with her. She speaks with him.*
→ Sie sprechen miteinander.	*They speak with one another.*

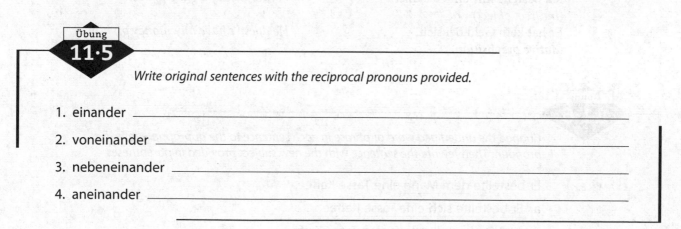

Übung 11·4

*Combine the following pairs of sentences by using a form of **einander**.*

1. Der Mann küsst die Frau. Die Frau küsst den Mann.

   _____

2. Martin will Heinz besuchen. Heinz will Martin besuchen.

   _____

3. Frau Keller fragte nach Herrn Benz. Herr Benz fragte nach Frau Keller.

   _____

4. Der Franzose wollte mit dem Schaffner sprechen. Der Schaffner wollte mit dem Franzosen sprechen.

   _____

Übung 11·5

Write original sentences with the reciprocal pronouns provided.

1. einander _____

2. voneinander _____

3. nebeneinander _____

4. aneinander _____

Reflexive pronouns

The reflexive pronoun **sich** is used with all third person pronouns and all nouns. It is only in the first and second persons that other forms occur, with certain differences between the accusative and dative cases:

NOM.	ACC.	DAT.	
ich	mich	mir	*I, myself*
du	dich	dir	*you, yourself*
er	sich	sich	*he, himself*
sie	sich	sich	*she, herself*
es	sich	sich	*it, itself*
wir	uns	uns	*we, ourselves*
ihr	euch	euch	*you, yourselves*
Sie	sich	sich	*you, yourself, yourselves*
sie	sich	sich	*they, themselves*

When the subject of a sentence and the pronoun object of that sentence refer to different persons or things, a reflexive pronoun is *not* used:

Der Mann fragte **sie**, wie es geschehen ist.   *The man asked her how it happened.*

But when the subject and object are the same person or thing, a reflexive pronoun is used:

Der Mann fragte **sich**, wie es geschehen ist.   *The man asked himself how it happened.*

If the pronoun object is a direct object or follows an accusative preposition, use the accusative reflexive pronoun. If the pronoun object is an indirect object or follows a dative preposition, use the dative reflexive pronoun:

Accusative
Wofür interessiert sie sich?   *What's she interested in?*
(*direct object*)
Du denkst nur an dich.   *You only think about yourself.*
(*accusative preposition*)

Dative
Ich bestelle mir ein Glas Bier.   *I order myself a glass of beer.*
(*indirect object*)
Er hat kein Geld bei sich.   *He doesn't have any money on him.*
(*dative preposition*)

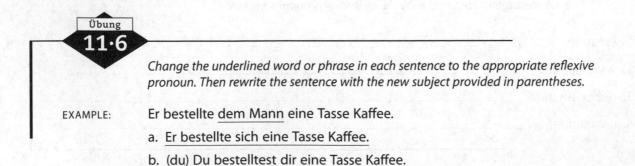

Übung
11·6

Change the underlined word or phrase in each sentence to the appropriate reflexive pronoun. Then rewrite the sentence with the new subject provided in parentheses.

EXAMPLE: Er bestellte <u>dem Mann</u> eine Tasse Kaffee.

a. <u>Er bestellte sich eine Tasse Kaffee.</u>

b. (du) <u>Du bestelltest dir eine Tasse Kaffee.</u>

1. Sie kauft den Kindern neue Schuhe.

   a. _____

   b. (wir) _____

2. Sie können mir nicht helfen.

   a. _____

   b. (ihr) _____

3. Er hat ihn gewaschen.

   a. _____

   b. (wer?) _____

4. Das wird er seinem Bruder nie verzeihen.

   a. _____

   b. (ich) _____

Übung

11·7

Write original sentences with the verb and the appropriate reflexive form of the pronoun provided.

EXAMPLE: kämmen, er <u>Er kämmt sich die Haare.</u>

1. finden, du _____

2. freuen, sie (*singular*) _____

3. bewegen, es _____

4. vorstellen, wir _____

Infinitives

Infinitives are the base form of verbs, which make up a significant component of a sentence. You are certainly aware of how to change an infinitive into a conjugated verb in the various tenses.

INFINITIVE	CONJUGATION	PRESENT PARTICIPLE	PAST PARTICIPLE
lachen	er lacht	lachend	gelacht

But infinitives play a larger role than just existing as a form that can be changed by verb endings.

Future tense

An infinitive can be a part of a future tense conjugation. Although the future tense can be *implied* by a present tense conjugation, the actual future tense is formed from a conjugation of **werden** plus an infinitive at the end of the clause. Note that the singular conjugation of **werden** is irregular in the second and third persons:

Ich werde es lesen.	*I will read it.*
Du wirst ihn besuchen.	*You will visit him.*
Er wird zu Hause bleiben.	*He will stay home.*

The plural conjugation follows a regular pattern:

Wir werden es verkaufen.	*We will sell it.*
Ihr werdet wieder gesund sein.	*You will be well again.*
Sie werden mitkommen.	*You will come along.*
Sie werden morgen abfahren.	*They will depart tomorrow.*

Modal auxiliaries

The infinitive, however, is used in other structures besides the future tense. Significant among these is its use with modal auxiliaries:

dürfen	*may, to be allowed to*
können	*can, to be able to*
mögen	*to like*
müssen	*must, to have to*
sollen	*should*
wollen	*to want*

In the present and past tenses, the modal is conjugated and the clause ends with an infinitive:

modal auxiliary + complement + infinitive
Ich muss + zu Hause + bleiben.
I have to stay home.

Present tense

Ich muss auf ihn warten.	*I have to wait for him.*
Das darfst du nicht tun.	*You're not allowed to do that.*

Past tense

Sie konnte ihn kaum verstehen.	*She could hardly understand him.*
Tina wollte Lehrerin werden.	*Tina wanted to become a teacher.*
Er sollte früher aufstehen.	*He should get up earlier.*

You should be aware that **mögen** has a high-frequency usage as *would like*, where it is conjugated in the subjunctive:

Subjunctive

Erik möchte mitkommen.	*Erik would like to come along.*

In the perfect and future tenses, a so-called *double infinitive* structure occurs at the end of the clause, with the modal auxiliary following its partner infinitive:

Sie hat es nicht lesen wollen.	*She didn't want to read it.*
Das hättest du nicht sagen sollen.	*You shouldn't have said that.*
Er wird nicht mitfahren dürfen.	*He won't be allowed to go along.*

When a double infinitive structure occurs in a subordinate clause (following conjunctions such as **dass**, **weil**, **ob**, and so on), the conjugated verb stands directly in front of the double infinitive:

Ich wusste nicht, dass sie es nicht hat lesen wollen.	*I didn't know that she didn't want to read it.*
Sie war empört, weil du es nicht hättest sagen sollen.	*She was outraged, because you shouldn't have said that.*
Weißt du, ob er wird mitfahren dürfen?	*Do you know if he will be allowed to go along?*

This kind of word order in subordinate clauses is also used with all other double infinitive structures that will be described in this chapter.

Lassen

When the verb **lassen** stands alone in a sentence, its meaning is *to let* or *leave*. But **lassen** can be used together with an infinitive. In such a case, its meaning is *to have* or *get*. For example:

Lass den Kindern den Spaß!	*Let the children have their fun.*
Ich lasse meinen Wagen reparieren.	*I get my car repaired.*
Ließ sie sich ein neues Kleid machen?	*Did she have a new dress made?*

And when it is used with the reflexive **sich**, **lassen** has a passive meaning, which in English often includes the meaning *can*. In this passive structure, the verbal element is again an infinitive and not a participle:

Solche Probleme lassen sich nicht leicht lösen.	*Such problems are not easily solved.*
Es ließ sich nicht beweisen.	*It wasn't proved.*
Das hat sich nicht leugnen lassen.	*It couldn't be denied.*

As with the modal auxiliaries, **lassen** in the present and past tenses is conjugated and the clause ends with an infinitive. In the perfect and future tenses, a double infinitive structure is required:

- Present or past tense

  modal or lassen + complement + infinitive
  Ich lasse + meinen Wagen + waschen.
  I have my car washed.

- Perfect or future tense

  auxiliary + complement + double infinitive
  Ich habe + meinen Wagen + waschen lassen.
  I have had my car washed.

Übung

12·1

Rewrite each of the following sentences with an appropriate modal auxiliary. Retain the tense of the original sentence.

EXAMPLE: Er verstand es nicht.

Er konnte es nicht verstehen.

1. Sein Vater trinkt kein Bier.

   _____

2. Die kranke Frau legte sich aufs Sofa.

   _____

3. Ich werde mich rasieren.

   _____

4. Der Kellner hat mir die Speisekarte und ein Glas Wasser gebracht.

   _____

5. Sie ging mit ihrem neuen Freund ins Theater.

   _____

6. Nach dem Essen sind wir in die Stadt gefahren.

   _____

7. Er macht am Wochenende mit seiner Freundin eine Fahrt nach Ulm.

   _____

*Follow the same directions as above, but add the verb **lassen** to each sentence instead of a modal auxiliary.*

1. Frau Benz hat das zerbrochene Fenster repariert.

   _____

2. Wir werden ein neues Haus im Vorort bauen.

   _____

3. Ich grüsste einen alten Freund.

   _____

4. Die Mädchen machten es aus Holz.

   _____

Compose sentences using the words provided in each list. Add any necessary words.

EXAMPLE: morgen / kommen / er / mit / Freund / nach Hause
             Morgen kommt er mit einem Freund nach Hause.

1. Problem / sich lassen / kaum / lösen

   _____

2. dies / zwei / Fenster / sich lassen / nicht / leicht / öffnen

   _____

3. können / du / ich / sagen / wo / du / Röcke / machen / lassen

   _____

4. Martin / sagen / dass / Freundin / Wagen / haben / kaufen / wollen

   _____

Helfen, hören, lehren, lernen, sehen

Just like the modal auxiliaries and **lassen**, the verbs **helfen**, **hören**, **lehren**, **lernen**, and **sehen** are conjugated in the present and past tenses and can be followed by an infinitive at the end of the clause. These verbs also require a double infinitive structure in the perfect and future tenses. Let's look at some example sentences:

Tina hilft mir die Sätze übersetzen.	*Tina helps me translate the sentences.*
Sie wird mir arbeiten helfen.	*She will help me work.*
Hörtest du die Nachtigall singen?	*Did you hear the nightingale singing?*
Wir haben die Männer sprechen hören.	*We heard the men talking.*
Frau Kamps lehrt uns schreiben.	*Ms. Kamps teaches us to write.*
Wer hat euch lesen lehren?	*Who taught you to read?*
Ich sah die Bauern auf dem Feld arbeiten.	*I saw the farmers working in the field.*
Er hat sie Karten spielen sehen.	*He saw them playing cards.*

Complete each line with an appropriate infinitive phrase.

1. Unsere Nachbarn helfen uns ...

_____

2. Sehen Sie den Gärtner ... ?

_____

3. Die Kinder hören die Mutter ...

_____

4. Mit der Zeit lernte das Kind ...

_____

5. Niemand lehrte sie ...

_____

6. Der alte Hund hörte ...

_____

7. Wer lehrt euch ... ?

_____

Verbs of motion

Certain verbs of motion, in particular **gehen**, **fahren**, **kommen**, and **schicken**, follow the same pattern with infinitives at the end of a clause. For example:

Er ging sich die Haare kämmen.	*He went to comb his hair.*
Fahrt ihr nachmittags einkaufen?	*Do you go shopping in the afternoon?*
Kommt ihr heute schwimmen?	*Are you coming swimming today?*
Mein Vater schickt mich Ski laufen.	*My father sends me skiing.*

The four categories of verbs described here all conform to the same pattern when combined with an infinitive. However, the verbs of motion tend not to be used in the perfect or future tenses.

Complete each line with an appropriate infinitive phrase.

1. Der Lehrer schickt die Schüler …

   _____

2. Kommt ihr morgen … ?

   _____

3. Jeden Freitag fuhren wir …

   _____

4. Die Touristen kamen …

   _____

Compose sentences using the words provided in each list. Add any necessary words.

EXAMPLE: morgen / helfen / er / wir / arbeiten

   <u>Morgen hilft er uns arbeiten.</u>

1. sein / Eltern / müssen / böse / Hund / wegjagen

   _____

2. unser / Onkel / mögen / gern / gut / Wein / trinken

   _____

3. haben / du / er / in / Schlafzimmer / kommen / hören / ?

   _____

4. mein / Tante / schicken / ich / oft / zu / Einkaufszentrum / einkaufen

   _____

Compose original sentences with the pairs of words provided.

EXAMPLE: wollen / helfen

Der Mann wollte der alten Frau helfen.

1. hören / singen

_____

2. müssen / reisen

_____

3. schicken / einkaufen

_____

4. sehen / spielen

_____

5. lernen / lesen

_____

6. kommen / Schlittschuh laufen

_____

7. lassen / reinigen

_____

Short responses

In every language there are little words that are added to sentences for emphasis or to give a particular quality to a phrase. There is only a slight difference of emphasis between the following two sentences, and it is the addition of one small adverb that causes this difference, and also adds a bit of indignation:

> *I don't know.*
> *I certainly don't know.*

German has numerous such small words, and this chapter will explain some of the important ones.

There are also in every language short, pat phrases used as a quick response to someone else's statement. They usually stand alone, because they derive their meaning from the statement to which they are responding. In English, the words *so what* and *how come* have little meaning when they stand alone, but as a response to something else, they can make quite a statement:

> —*You didn't make your bed again.*   —*So what!*
> —*You're grounded for a week!*   —*How come?*

The same thing occurs in German. And these short, pat responses are effective in sentence writing, because they make the language flow naturally and can make content more interesting. However, such phrases are often quite casual and should sometimes be avoided in formal writing.

Words for emphasis

German often adds special words to a sentence in order to emphasize a speaker's or a writer's attitude or frame of mind: impatience, enthusiasm, indignation, and so on.

Also

The word **also** (*so, well*) is usually added to a phrase to emphasize the urgency of the action of a verb or as a way of linking a phrase to a previous statement.

Also schön!	*All right then!*
Na also!	*You see! (I told you so!)*
Also, kommt er jetzt oder nicht?	*Well, is he coming or not?*

Doch

Doch can be used alone as a response that says that what someone else has suggested is not true:

Du hast den Aufsatz noch nicht geschrieben!	*You haven't written the essay yet!*
Doch!	*Yes, I have!*

It is also added to a phrase to emphasize its meaning:

Los doch!	*Go ahead! Go on already!*
Das ist doch herrlich!	*That's really great!*
Das ist doch eine Lüge!	*That's such a lie!*

Gar

Gar usually means *at all* but can also be added to a phrase for emphasis:

Magst du Tee trinken?	*Do you like drinking tea?*
Gar nicht.	*Not at all.*
Hast du genug Euro?	*Do you have enough euros?*
Nein, ich habe gar keine.	*No, I have none at all.*
Tina ist wirklich hübsch.	*Tina is really pretty.*
Ja, ich hätte gar zu gern mit ihr getanzt.	*Yes, I really would have liked to dance with her.*

Kaum

The word **kaum** is an adverb and means *hardly* or *scarcely*. But it is added to other phrases to emphasize the moment when something occurs:

Sie hatte kaum Platz genommen, da sie fing an zu weinen.	*She had hardly taken her seat when she began to cry.*

It is often used to modify a comparative:

Der Professor ist kaum älter als die Studenten.	*The professor is hardly older than the students.*
Das ist kaum besser!	*That's hardly better!*

It is also frequently combined with an infinitive clause introduced by **zu**:

Kaum zu glauben.	*It's hard to believe.*
Seine Handschrift ist kaum zu entziffern.	*His handwriting can hardly be made out.*

Mal

The word **mal** is a shortened version of the word **einmal** (*once*). It is often added to a phrase—particularly an imperative—for emphasis:

Komm mal her!	*Come here.*
Hört mal zu!	*Listen up!*
Hör mal damit auf!	*Stop it!*

Wie

The interrogative **wie** (*how*) is often combined with other words to form a variety of pat phrases. Many are questions that begin with *how*:

Wie oft geht ihr ins Kino?	*How often do you go to the movies?*
Wie viel kostet so ein Auto?	*How much does a car like that cost?*
Wie spät ist es?	*What time is it?*

Wie is also used in other expressions:

Wie bitte?	*What? / I beg your pardon.*
Wieso denn?	*Why?*
Und wie!	*And how!*
Wie war das?	*What did you say?*
Wie das?	*How did that happen?*

Zwar

The adverb **zwar** means *indeed* or *admittedly* and is used to stress a point in a statement or to admit to involvement in a circumstance:

Ich weiß es zwar nicht genau, aber ich nehme es als die Wahrheit an.	*I admit I'm not really sure, but I accept it as the truth.*
Onkel Karl kommt morgen, und zwar vor Mittag.	*Uncle Karl is coming tomorrow, and indeed before noon.*
Sie ist Richterin und zwar eine gute.	*She's a judge, and a good one at that.*

Übung
13·1

*Fill in the blank of each sentence with an appropriate word from the following list: **also, doch, gar, kaum, mal, wie,** or **zwar**.*

1. _____ schnell kann das Pferd laufen?

2. Erik kennt sie _____ nicht, aber er sieht sie jeden Tag an der Ecke stehen.

3. _____ zu glauben!

4. Der hochnäsige Student ist _____ nicht so intelligent.

5. Der Dieb ist _____ auch ein Lügner!

6. _____, bis morgen. Schlaf gut!

7. „Du hast deine Handschuhe wieder verloren!" „_____ nicht!"

*Write original sentences with **also**, **doch**, **gar**, **kaum**, **mal**, **wie**, and **zwar**.*

1. also _____

2. doch _____

3. gar _____

4. mal _____

5. kaum _____

6. wie _____

7. zwar _____

Pat phrases

There are numerous short phrases that are pat responses to someone else's remarks. The following list contains some of the most frequently used ones:

Ausgezeichnet!	*Excellent!*
Das ist nicht zu glauben.	*That's unbelievable.*
Das kommt darauf an.	*That depends.*
Donnerwetter!	*For Heaven's sake!*
Du spinnst!	*You're crazy! You're nuts!*
Erstaunlich!	*Astounding!*
Großartig!	*Great!*
Keine Ahnung.	*I have no idea.*
Keine Ursache.	*Don't mention it.*
Leider nicht.	*Unfortunately, not.*
Natürlich.	*Naturally.*
Offenbar.	*Obviously. Clearly.*
Offensichtlich.	*Obviously.*
Scheinbar.	*Apparently. So it seems.*
Selbstverständlich.	*Of course.*
Super!	*Super!*
Tatsächlich?	*Really?*
Toll!	*Terrific!*
Überhaupt nicht.	*Not at all.*
Unglaublich.	*Incredible.*
Unmöglich.	*Impossible.*
Wunderbar!	*Wonderful!*

It is possible to use more than one of these expressions as a response to a particular remark. Let's look at a few example sentences that illustrate which responses are appropriate for the meaning of each sentence:

Wir gehen morgen Rad fahren.   *We're going bike riding tomorrow.*
→   Großartig!
Super!
Tatsächlich?

Herr Schneider wurde gestern verhaftet.   *Mr. Schneider was arrested yesterday.*
→   Das ist nicht zu glauben!
Donnerwetter!
Tatsächlich?

Willst du mir malen helfen?   *Do you want to help me paint?*
→   Das kommt darauf an.
Leider nicht.
Überhaupt nicht.

Fill in the blank following each sentence with an appropriate pat response.

1. Gestern abend ist mein erster Sohn geboren.

   _____

2. Ich habe eine neue Art Computer erfunden.

   _____

3. Wir haben den ganzen Tag auf der Terrasse sonnengebadet.

   _____

4. Kommt der nächste Zug um 22 Uhr?

   _____

5. Du hast 100.000 Euro gewonnen!

   _____

6. Ist Ihre Mutter wieder gesund geworden?

   _____

7. Hast du Lust eine Fahrt nach Paris zu machen?

   _____

Write a sentence that is appropriate for the response given.

EXAMPLE: <u>Hast du deine Handtasche gefunden?</u>
Leider nicht.

1. _____

Das kommt darauf an.

2. _____

Tatsächlich?

3. _____

Keine Ahnung.

4. _____

Wunderbar!

5. _____

Scheinbar.

6. _____

Erstaunlich!

7. _____

Toll!

Idioms and special phrases

Idioms are phrases that acquire their meaning from an entire expression and cannot be translated word for word. Imagine a German trying to make sense of the phrase *Good looks run in the family* by checking out the individual words in a dictionary.

ordinary words + unexpected usage → idiom

The same is true when dealing with German idioms. Although they require care in their use, idioms are highly useful for writing interesting sentences, because they often provide a casual tone to a sentence and even a little fun in a text.

Not all phrases that are difficult to translate are idioms. Some just have a special or even limited usage or are part of the German grammar that does not exist in English.

Let's look at a variety of idioms and special phrases that can be useful in creating lively or colorful sentences. Some are pat phrases that have only one form; others are more flexible and can change elements within their structure.

Gern

The verb *to like* in German is composed of the infinitive **haben** followed by **gern**:

Hast du ihn gern?	*Do you like him?*
Tina hat Professor Keller gern.	*Tina likes Professor Keller.*

Gern can be used with other verbs and still retain the meaning *like*. In such cases the word **gern** follows the verb directly and is not at the end of the clause as with **haben**:

Ich tanze gern mit Angela.	*I like dancing with Angela.*
Die Mädchen spielen gern Tennis oder Basketball.	*The girls like playing tennis or basketball.*

The comparative and superlative of **gern** are **lieber** and **am liebsten**, respectively, and show a higher degree of liking to do something:

Wir spielen lieber Schach.	*We prefer to play chess.*
Wir spielen am liebsten Tennis.	*Most of all we like to play tennis.*

Write original sentences with **gern haben**, using the given cues.

EXAMPLE: der neue Lehrer <u>Haben Sie den neuen Lehrer nicht gern?</u>

1. der neue Student _____

2. Frau Schneider _____

3. du _____

4. diese betrunkenen Männer _____

*Now use the given verbs as your cues for writing original sentences with **gern**.*

EXAMPLE: spielen <u>Ich spiele gern Ziehharmonika.</u>

5. wandern

_____

6. reisen

_____

7. sich ausruhen

_____

Useful expressions

The following structure contains the modal **sollen** and can be used with a wide variety of verbs:

hätte + infinitive + sollen
Ich hätte es + tun + sollen.
I should have done it.

Das hättest du nicht sagen sollen.	*You shouldn't have said that.*
Das hätte man nicht tun sollen.	*One shouldn't have done that.*
Er hätte die Flasche Bier langsamer trinken sollen.	*He should have drunk the bottle of beer slower.*

A variety of subjects can be used with the following expression:

Die ganze Familie ist vor die Hunde gegangen.	*The whole family went to the dogs.*
Unser Geschäft wird vor die Hunde gehen.	*Our business will go to the dogs.*
Der alte Mann ist vor die Hunde gegangen.	*The old man kicked the bucket.*

Numerous noun phrases or pronouns can follow the preposition **auf** in the expression that follows and means *to look forward to* something (don't confuse it with **sich freuen über**, which means *to be happy about* something):

Er freut sich aufs Wochenende.	*He's looking forward to the weekend.*
Wir freuen uns auf unseren Urlaub.	*We're looking forward to our vacation.*
Freuen Sie sich nicht darauf?	*Aren't you looking forward to it?*

You can use any number of infinitive phrases to follow **Lust haben**:

Hast du Lust ins Kino zu gehen?	*Do you feel like going to the movies?*
Habt ihr Lust in die Stadt zu fahren?	*Do you feel like driving into the city?*
Ich habe keine Lust dazu.	*I don't feel like it.*

Expressions with **satt haben** and **leiden** can use many different kinds of direct objects:

Ich habe es satt.	*I'm sick of it.*
Ich habe dein Benehmen wirklich satt.	*I'm really fed up with your behavior.*
Sie hat ihren ehemaligen Mann satt.	*She's fed up with her former husband.*

Ich kann den Mann nicht leiden.	*I can't stand the man.*
Kannst du solche Musik auch nicht leiden?	*Can't you stand that kind of music either?*
Meine Frau kann meinen neuen Chef nicht leiden.	*My wife can't stand my new boss.*

A few different prepositional phrases can be used with the verb **sich auskennen**:

Kennt er sich in dieser Stadt aus?	*Does he know his way around this city?*
Tanja kennt sich bei den Männern aus.	*Tanja knows a lot about men.*
Kennen Sie sich mit der klassischen Periode aus?	*Are you familiar with the classical period?*

A variety of objects can follow **mit** when using the verb **übereinstimmen**:

Sie stimmt mit mir überein.	*She agrees with me.*
Ich kann nicht mit Herrn Benz übereinstimmen.	*I can't agree with Mr. Benz.*

Übung

14·2

Rewrite each sentence, changing the underlined element to the cue in parentheses.

EXAMPLE: Ich stimme mit <u>Erik</u> überein.

(ihr) <u>Ich stimme mit euch überein.</u>

1. Ich habe <u>ihn</u> nicht gern.

   a. (diese Frau) _____

   b. (solche Leute) _____

2. Das hättest <u>du</u> nicht fragen sollen.

   a. (ihr) _____

   b. (Sie) _____

3. <u>Die ganze Familie</u> wird vor die Hunde gehen.

   a. (sein Vater) _____

   b. (diese Pläne) _____

4. Ich freue mich schon auf <u>unseren Urlaub</u>.

   a. (dein Aufenthalt in Bremen) _____

   b. (euer Besuch) _____

5. Hast du Lust <u>mexikanisch zu essen</u>?

   a. (Du besuchst Freunde in der Stadt.) _____

   b. (Du siehst fern.) _____

6. Ich habe <u>diese Musik</u> wirklich satt!

   a. (diese dummen Witze) _____

   b. (deine andauernden Fragen) _____

Some idioms and special phrases tend to be used in a singular way, with only the subject or tense of the phrase occasionally changing:

Achtung, fertig, los!	On your mark, get set, go!
Armer Kerl.	Poor guy.
Besser spät als nie.	Better late than never.
Das ist doch reiner Quatsch!	That's utter nonsense!
Du musst den Kopf hoch tragen.	You have to hold your head up high.
Du nimmst mich auf den Arm.	You're pulling my leg.
Er ist diese Woche nicht bei Kasse.	He's short on cash this week.
Er ist seinem Vater wie aus dem Gesicht geschnitten.	He's a chip off the old block.
Er war bis über beide Ohren in sie verliebt.	He was head over heels in love with her.
Es macht mir nichts aus.	It doesn't matter to me.
Frische dein Deutsch auf!	Brush up on your German.
Gib Acht!	Pay attention.
Halt den Mund!	Shut up!
Hau ab!	Knock it off! / Get out!
Ich gebe dir eine Ohrfeige!	I'll give you a good smack!
Ich habe mit dir ein Hühnchen zu rupfen.	I've got a bone to pick with you.
Ich war in der Klemme!	I was in a real fix.
Kopf oder Zahl?	Heads or tails?
Mir war hundeelend.	I was sick as a dog.
Nimm dich zusammen!	Get a grip!
o-beinig/x-beinig	bowlegged/knock-kneed
Prima.	Terrific.
Seine Frau ist wieder in andern Umständen.	His wife's in the family way again.
Setz dich nicht aufs hohe Pferd!	Get off your high horse!
Sie können Gift darauf nehmen.	You can bet your bottom dollar on it.
so viel ich weiß	as far as I know
übrigens	by the way

um so besser	all the better
Verschwinde!	Get out of here!
von Kopf bis Fuß	from head to toe
Wie immer schwatzt er.	As usual, he's talking a lot of hot air.

Übung

14·3

Write an original statement that would provoke the response that follows.

EXAMPLE: <u>Warum hast du so lange geschlafen?</u>

Mir war hundeelend.

1. _____

Nein! Ich kann ihn nicht leiden!

2. _____

Besser spät als nie.

3. _____

Der arme Kerl ist o-beinig.

4. _____

Es macht mir nichts aus.

5. _____

So viel ich weiß.

6. _____

Von Kopf bis Fuß.

7. _____

Setz dich nicht aufs hohe Pferd!

Übung

14·4

Using one of the idioms or special phrases discussed above, write a response to each of the following statements.

EXAMPLE: Wir wollen darum losen.

<u>Kopf oder Zahl?</u>

1. Erik sagt, dass sein Vater reich ist und seine Mutter eine Schönheitskönigin ist.

_____

2. Wollen sie denn noch mehr Kinder?

_____

3. Ich habe neulich 200 Euro gewonnen!

_____

4. Warum kann Martin nicht mit uns reisen?

_____

Reflexive verbs in special phrases

Certain German expressions require a reflexive verb. The following examples illustrate the use of reflexives in sentences and how the English translation of those sentences does not necessarily contain a reflexive:

Beeile dich!	_Hurry up!_
Die Firma will sich von ihm trennen.	_The company wants to let him go._
Die Kinder fürchten sich vor dir.	_The children are afraid of you._
Er hat sich schlecht benommen.	_He behaved badly._
Er versucht sich ruhig zu verhalten.	_He tries to keep quiet._
Erinnerst du dich daran?	_Do you remember it?_
Ich kann mich nicht an die neue Wohnung gewöhnen.	_I can't get used to the new apartment._
Martin hat sich zur Heirat entschlossen.	_Martin decided to get married._
Sie hat sich gegen die Idee entschieden.	_She decided against the idea._
Sie hat sich sehr bemüht.	_She really tried hard._

The reflexive pronoun occurs after the conjugated verb in a declarative sentence and after the subject in an interrogative sentence.

Übung 14·5

Rewrite each of the following phrases by changing the underlined word or phrase to the cue given in parentheses. Then change the underlined element to something of your own choosing.

EXAMPLE: Sie hat sich sehr bemüht.

a. (Erik) Erik hat sich sehr bemüht.

b. Die Kinder haben sich sehr bemüht.

1. Beeile dich!

a. (ihr) _____

b. _____

2. Die Firma will sich von ihm trennen.

a. (Herr Keller) _____

b. _____

3. Die Kinder fürchten sich vor dir.

   a. (deine Frau) _____

   b. _____

4. Er hat sich schlecht benommen.

   a. (mit Tapferkeit) _____

   b. _____

5. Erinnerst du dich daran?

   a. (Sie) _____

   b. _____

6. Ich kann mich nicht an die neue Wohnung gewöhnen.

   a. (das laute Bellen) _____

   b. _____

7. Martin hat sich zur Heirat entschlossen.

   a. (ich) _____

   b. _____

Antonyms and contrasts

Antonyms are pairs of words that have meanings opposite to each other, such as *black* and *white* or *large* and *small*. In addition to antonyms, there are other pairs of words or phrases that are merely contrasts and not true opposites. But, like antonyms, they are useful in helping to create interesting sentences.

links ← Gegensätze → **rechts**

left ←antonyms → *right*

Some antonyms and contrasts take the form of verbs. Let's look at some:

ankommen / abfahren	*arrive / depart*
erlauben / verbieten	*allow / forbid*
essen / verhungern	*eat / starve*
geben / nehmen	*give / take*
helfen / behindern	*help / hinder*
kaputt machen / reparieren	*break / repair*
kaufen / verkaufen	*buy / sell*
kommen / gehen	*come / go*
lachen / weinen	*laugh / cry*
leben / sterben	*live / die*
lieben / hassen	*love / hate*
schicken / bekommen	*send / receive*
spielen / arbeiten	*play / work*
stolz sein / sich schämen	*be proud / be ashamed*
trinken / verdursten	*drink / die of thirst*

Übung
15·1

Write a negative response to each of the following questions by using the antonym or contrasting verb of the one found in the question.

EXAMPLE: Liebst du den Mann?

Nein. Überhaupt nicht. Ich hasse ihn.

1. Hast du diese große Flasche Wasser getrunken?

_____

2. Sind die Touristen heute morgen angekommen?

_____

3. Wirst du deiner Tante ein Geburtstagsgeschenk schicken?

_____

4. Hat dein Vater dir erlaubt ein neues Fahrrad zu kaufen?

_____

5. Weint Frau Weber wieder?

_____

6. Essen die Flüchtlinge jenes Landes genug Obst und Gemüse?

_____

7. Wird jemand euer Haus kaufen?

_____

8. Kommst du zur Schule?

_____

9. Hassen Sie klassische Musik?

_____

10. Hast du den Brief von Martin bekommen?

_____

Some antonyms are nouns:

Ebene / Berg	*plain / mountain*
Freude / Zorn	*joy / anger*
Gefangenschaft / Freiheit	*imprisonment / freedom*
Gott / Teufel	*God / devil*
Herr / Dame	*gentleman / lady*
Himmel / Hölle	*heaven / hell*
Junge / Mädchen	*boy / girl*
Kälte / Hitze	*cold / heat*
Kind / Erwachsene	*child / adult*
Komödie / Tragödie	*comedy / tragedy*
Krankheit / Gesundheit	*sickness / health*
Krieg / Frieden	*war / peace*
Leben / Tod	*life / death*
Lehrling / Meister	*apprentice / supervisor*
Liebe / Hass	*love / hate*
Mann / Frau	*man, husband / woman, wife*
Reichtum / Armut	*wealth / poverty*
Spitze / Sohle	*top / bottom*
Tag / Nacht	*day / night*
Vorderseite / Rückseite	*front / rear*

Using each pair of noun antonyms previously listed, write a question that asks for a comparison between the two nouns.

EXAMPLE: Ist Reichtum wirklich besser als Armut?

1. _____
2. _____
3. _____
4. _____
5. _____
6. _____
7. _____
8. _____
9. _____
10. _____
11. _____
12. _____
13. _____
14. _____
15. _____
16. _____
17. _____
18. _____
19. _____
20. _____

There are many pairs of adjective and adverb antonyms and contrasting pairs:

dunkel / hell	*dark / bright*
einfach / kompliziert	*simple / complicated*
erfahren / unerfahren	*experienced / inexperienced*
faul / fleißig	*lazy / diligent*
früh / spät	*early / late*
gebildet / unwissend	*educated / ignorant*
glänzend / matt	*shiny / dull*
groß / klein	*big / little*

gut / schlecht	good / bad
hässlich / hübsch	ugly / beautiful
heiß / kalt	hot / cold
hungrig / satt	hungry / satiated
interessant / langweilig	interesting / boring
kaltblütig / warmblütig	cold-blooded / warm-blooded
lang / kurz	long / short
langsam / schnell	slow / fast
laut / leise	loud / quiet
leicht / schwer	easy, light / hard, heavy
reich / arm	rich / poor
sauber / schmutzig	clean / dirty
schwarz / weiß	black / white
stabil / wackelig	steady / wobbly
stark / schwach	strong / weak
traurig / glücklich	sad / happy
trocken / nass	dry / wet

Write a statement that says that someone or something isn't "x," but rather "y," using the adjective/adverb antonym pairs listed above.

EXAMPLE: schwarz <u>Diese Katze ist nicht schwarz, sondern weiß.</u>

1. schwach _____

2. wackelig _____

3. hell _____

4. unerfahren _____

5. trocken _____

6. schmutzig _____

7. satt _____

8. glänzend _____

9. warmblütig _____

10. fleißig _____

Comparative and superlative

Adjective and adverb pairs of antonyms and contrasts do not occur solely in the positive form. They also have a comparative form and a superlative form. (See Chapter 9 for the formation and use of comparative and superlative adjectives and adverbs.) When adjectives are used as predicate adjectives, the comparative has no ending, and the superlative appears in a prepositional phrase introduced by **am**:

Positive

Unser Haus ist klein.	*Our house is little.*
Die Schule ist groß.	*The school is big.*

Comparative

Unser Haus ist kleiner.	*Our house is littler.*
Die Schule ist größer.	*The school is bigger.*

Superlative

Unser Haus ist am kleinsten.	*Our house is the littlest.*
Die Schule ist am größten.	*The school is the biggest.*

But when a comparative or superlative adjective is declined, just like a positive adjective it must have the appropriate adjective endings:

Positive

Der alte Mann ist krank. (*nom.*)	*The old man is sick.*
Kennst du den jungen Mann? (*acc.*)	*Do you know the young man?*

Comparative

Er hilft dem älteren Mann. (*dat.*)	*He helps the older man.*
Das ist der Pass des jüngeren Mannes. (*gen.*)	*That's the younger man's passport.*

Superlative

Es ist für den ältesten Mann. (*acc.*)	*It's for the oldest man.*
Der jüngste Mann muss hier bleiben. (*nom.*)	*The youngest man must remain here.*

Adverbs in the positive and comparative forms require no endings. But in the superlative, they appear in a prepositional phrase introduced by **am**:

Positive

Erik arbeitet schnell.	*Erik works fast.*
Warum fährt der Zug langsam?	*Why is the train moving slowly?*

Comparative

Kannst du nicht schneller arbeiten?	*Can't you work faster?*
Der Ausländer spricht langsamer.	*The foreigner speaks more slowly.*

Superlative

Sabine läuft am schnellsten.	*Sabine runs the fastest.*
Der Junge schreibt am langsamsten.	*The boy writes the slowest.*

Adjectives and adverbs that have an umlaut vowel (**a**, **o**, or **u**) often require an umlaut on that vowel in the comparative and superlative.

A note of caution: English has two ways of forming the comparative and superlative. One is similar to the German (*big, bigger, biggest*). The other way is to precede an adjective or adverb with the words *more* or *most*. This happens when the English adjective or adverb is a long word or comes from a foreign source. For example:

interesting	*more interesting*	*most interesting*
ridiculous	*more ridiculous*	*most ridiculous*
superficial	*more superficial*	*most superficial*

When writing German sentences, be aware of the two kinds of English comparative and superlative and remember that German has only one form:

kleiner / am kleinsten   smaller / smallest
schöner / am schönsten   more beautiful / most beautiful

Übung 15·4

Using the adjectives or adverbs provided as cues, write original sentences that compare two people or things.

EXAMPLE: alt <u>Onkel Benno ist viel älter als Tante Marianne.</u>

1. klug _____

2. komisch _____

3. eingebildet _____

4. hoch _____

5. lerneifrig _____

6. wackelig _____

7. dunkel _____

8. schrecklich _____

9. preiswert _____

10. artig _____

Übung 15·5

Using the three elements provided as cues, write two original sentences with pairs of contrasting adjectives or adverbs of your choice. Use a comparative in your first sentence and a superlative in your second sentence.

EXAMPLE: Vater, Mutter, Großvater

    a. <u>Mein Vater ist ein bisschen jünger als meine Mutter.</u>

    b. <u>Mein Großvater ist am ältesten.</u>

1. Tulpen, Nelken, Rosen

  a. _____

  b. _____

2. Igel, Katze, Löwe

  a. _____

  b. _____

3. Milchladen, Rathaus, Dom

   a. _____

   b. _____

4. Schüler, Lehrerin, Professor

   a. _____

   b. _____

5. eine tropische Insel, Italien, Sibirien

   a. _____

   b. _____

6. Economywagen, VW, Mercedes Benz

   a. _____

   b. _____

7. Wurm, Klapperschlange, Anakonda

   a. _____

   b. _____

8. Essig, Sauerrahm, Pflaumenkuchen

   a. _____

   b. _____

9. Schlange, Wolf, Bär

   a. _____

   b. _____

10. Luftschiff, Doppeldecker, Düsenjäger

   a. _____

   b. _____

The passive voice

In German, the passive voice is a widely used structure. There are two forms of the passive voice. The first consists of a conjugation of the verb **werden** and a past participle:

> **werden + past participle**
> Es wird + gebrochen.
> *It is (being) broken.*

The active voice

But before looking at the passive voice, let's consider the active voice, which is essentially the parent of the passive voice. The active voice sentence is made up of a subject, a transitive verb, and a direct object, a combination of direct and indirect objects, or the object of a dative verb:

> **subject + transitive verb + object → active voice**
> Er hat den Richter gestört.   *He disturbed the judge.*
> Sie gibt dem Herrn ein Geschenk.   *She gives the man a gift.*
> Wir haben der Lehrerin gedankt.   *We thanked the teacher.*

The passive voice in German

The elements of the passive voice sentence are the conjugation of **werden** and a past participle. Let's look at the various tenses of the passive voice in the third person singular with the verb **lesen**:

Present:	wird gelesen	*is read*
Past:	wurde gelesen	*was read*
Present perfect:	ist gelesen worden	*has been read*
Past perfect:	war gelesen worden	*had been read*
Future:	wird gelesen werden	*will be read*

Notice that the perfect tenses use **worden** as the past participle of **werden**. This only occurs in the passive voice, in which **werden** is translated as *to be*. When **werden** means *to become* or *get*, its past participle is **geworden**.

If the active voice sentence has an accusative direct object, the passive voice sentence uses the direct object as its subject, which must be in the nominative case. The tense of the verb in the active sentence becomes the tense of the verb **werden** in the passive sentence. The active voice subject becomes the object of the preposition **von** in the passive sentence. And the verb in the active sentence is formed as a past participle in the passive sentence. For example:

Er stört den Richter.	*He disturbs the judge.*
Passive subject:	der Richter
Passive form of werden **in the present tense:**	wird
Passive object of von:	von ihm
Passive past participle:	gestört

The passive voice version of the sentence:

Der Richter wird von ihm gestört.   *The judge is disturbed by him.*

If the active sentence were in the past tense, the passive sentence would become:

Der Richter wurde von ihm gestört.   *The judge was disturbed by him.*

If it were in the present perfect tense, the passive sentence would become:

Der Richter ist von ihm gestört worden.   *The judge has been disturbed by him.*

And if it were in the future tense, the passive sentence would become:

Der Richter wird von ihm gestört werden.   *The judge will be disturbed by him.*

Übung
16·1

Rewrite the following passive sentences in the missing tenses.

1. *Present* Die Briefe werden von mir geschickt.

   a. *Past* _____

   b. *Present perfect* _____

   c. *Future* _____

2. a. *Present* _____

   Past Die Aufgaben wurden von den Schülern gemacht.

   b. *Present perfect* _____

   c. *Future* _____

3. *Present* Der Ball wird von den Kindern gesucht.

   a. *Past* _____

   b. *Present perfect* _____

   c. *Future* _____

4. a. *Present* _____

   b. *Past* _____

   Present perfect Eine neue Stadt ist von den Entdeckungsreisenden gegründet worden.

   c. *Future* _____

5. a. *Present* _____

   b. *Past* _____

   c. *Present perfect* _____

   Future Das Haus wird von den Arbeitern gebaut werden.

6. *Present* Dieses Fest wird von vielen Menschen gefeiert.

   a. *Past* _____

   b. *Present perfect* _____

   c. *Future* _____

7. a. *Present* _____

   Past Im 21. Jahrhundert wurden die ersten elektrischen Autos von ihnen gebaut.

   b. *Present perfect* _____

   c. *Future* _____

Übung
16·2

Change the following active sentences to the passive voice. Retain the tense of the original sentences.

EXAMPLE: Das Mädchen lernte das Gedicht auswendig.
             Das Gedicht wurde von dem Mädchen auswendig gelernt.

1. Die Lehrerin hat das Wort buchstabiert.

   _____

2. Herr Schneider fotografierte das riesige Düsenflugzeug.

   _____

3. Bomben haben das kleine Dorf zerstört.

   _____

4. Der Arzt wird ein Mittel gegen Heuschnupfen verschreiben.

   _____

5. Oft opfern mutige Männer das eigene Leben für die Wissenschaft.

   _____

6. Die Wirtin vermietete drei Einzelzimmer.

   _____

7. Im 15. Jahrhundert hat Gutenberg die Bibel gedruckt.

_____

8. Die Kellnerin bringt zwei Gläser Bier.

_____

9. Man hat ihren Geburtstag wieder vergessen.

_____

10. Der faule Sohn enttäuschte seine Eltern.

_____

11. Die Wissenschaftler werden niemals alle Krankheiten heilen.

_____

12. Die Professorin stellt den Diplomaten vor.

_____

13. Frau Doktor Keller hat den Vortrag gehalten.

_____

14. Die Ausländer brauchen viele Ansichtskarten.

_____

If an active sentence has both a direct object (accusative case) and an indirect object (dative case), it is only the direct object that can become the subject of the passive form of the active sentence. The indirect object remains in the dative case. However, the indirect object can be placed at the beginning of the sentence or it can follow the conjugated verb:

subject + werden + indirect object + past participle → passive sentence

or

indirect object + werden + subject + past participle → passive sentence

For example:

Active voice:	Tina hat ihm das Buch gegeben.	_Tina gave him the book._
Passive voice:	Das Buch ist ihm von Tina gegeben worden.	_The book was given to him by Tina._
	_or_ Ihm ist das Buch von Tina gegeben worden.	
Active voice:	Wir schickten einem Freund ein Geschenk.	_We sent a friend a gift._
Passive voice:	Ein Geschenk wurde einem Freund von uns geschickt.	_A gift was sent to a friend by us._
	_or_ Einem Freund wurde ein Geschenk von uns geschickt.	

Rewrite the following passive sentences in the missing tenses.

1. *Present* Jedem Schüler wird ein Bleistift von der Lehrerin gegeben.

   a. *Past* _____

   b. *Present perfect* _____

   c. *Future* _____

2. *a. Present* _____

   b. *Past* _____

   c. *Present perfect* _____

   Future Seinen Eltern wird ein CD-Player geschenkt werden.

3. a. *Present* _____

   Past Ihnen wurden die Bilder vom Reiseführer gezeigt.

   b. *Present perfect* _____

   c. *Future* _____

Change the following active sentences to the passive voice. Retain the tense of the original sentences.

EXAMPLE: Sie gibt mir zwei Bücher.

   <u>Mir werden zwei Bücher von ihr gegeben.</u>

1. Man brachte dem Kranken ein Kissen.

   _____

2. Die Reisenden senden ihnen Ansichtskarten.

   _____

3. Die Firma hat Herrn Braun die Waren ins Haus gesandt.

   _____

4. Wem geben die Mädchen diese Geschenke?

   _____

5. Meine Schwester hat dem neuen Studenten die Videos geliehen.

   _____

6. Was hat der Diplomat der Kanzlerin versprochen?

   _____

7. Was bringst du den Gastgebern?

_____

8. Die Professorin hat dem neuen Dozenten einen teuren Füller geschenkt.

_____

9. Der Torwart warf dem Stürmer den Ball.

_____

Dative objects in the passive voice

When the object of a dative verb in an active sentence is placed in a passive voice sentence, the object must remain in the dative case. The subject of the passive sentence will be the optional pronoun **es**, thus conjugating **werden** with a third person singular subject:

dative object + **werden** + **(es)** + past participle → passive sentence

For example:

Active voice:	Man glaubt ihm nicht.	_People don't believe him._
Passive voice:	Ihm wird nicht geglaubt.	_He isn't believed._
	(Es wird ihm nicht geglaubt.)	
Active voice:	Martin hat dem Mann gedankt.	_Martin thanked the man._
Passive voice:	Dem Mann ist von Martin gedankt worden.	_The man was thanked by Martin._

As with other passive voice sentences, the tense of **werden** in the passive sentence must be the tense of the verb in the active sentence, and that verb becomes a past participle in the passive voice sentence. If the verb **glauben** is in the past tense, the passive sentence becomes:

Ihm wurde nicht geglaubt.	_He wasn't believed._

If **glauben** is in the present perfect tense, the passive sentence becomes:

Ihm ist nicht geglaubt worden.	_He wasn't (hasn't been) believed._

If **glauben** is in the future tense, the passive sentence becomes:

Ihm wird nicht geglaubt werden.	_He won't be believed._

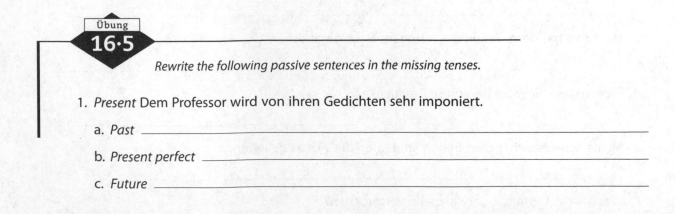

Übung

16·5

Rewrite the following passive sentences in the missing tenses.

1. _Present_ Dem Professor wird von ihren Gedichten sehr imponiert.

   a. _Past_ _____

   b. _Present perfect_ _____

   c. _Future_ _____

2. a. *Present* _____

   Past Dem Lehrer wurde nicht geantwortet.

   b. *Present perfect* _____

   c. *Future* _____

3. a. *Present* _____

   b. *Past* _____

   c. *Present perfect* _____

   Future Der Wirtin wird mit einer Geldstrafe gedroht werden.

If the subject of an active sentence is **man** (*one, you*) or another word that does not specify anyone in particular (*they, people, some,* and so on), that word can be omitted from the passive voice sentence: Active—**Man glaubte ihm nicht.** Passive—**Ihm wurde nicht geglaubt.**

Übung
16·6

Change the following active sentences to the passive voice. Retain the tense of the original sentences.

EXAMPLE: Er drohte ihr mit seinem Zeigefinger.

Ihr wurde von ihm mit seinem Zeigefinger gedroht.

1. Ein gutes Wörterbuch wird einem Germanisten nützen.

   _____

2. Man wird solchen Politikern nie vertrauen.

   _____

3. Man hat ihm kaum zugehört.

   _____

4. Haben die frechen Lehrlinge dem Meister widersprochen?

   _____

5. Das wird der Gerechtigkeit nicht dienen.

   _____

6. Der Trickbetrüger schmeichelte ihr andauernd.

   _____

7. Warum glauben sie mir nicht?

   _____

In a passive sentence, the preposition *of* is translated into German by either **von** or **durch**. **Von** is used most often when the "agent" of the action of the verb is a person, but also occurs when the agent is a natural cause or force of nature. **Durch** is used primarily with actions caused by a thing but also with actions caused by a person who acts as an intermediary. For example:

Person:	Der Roman wurde von Sabine gelesen.	*The novel was read by Sabine.*
Natural cause:	Das Dorf wird von einem Waldbrand bedroht.	*The village is threatened by a forest fire.*
Thing:	Die Epidemie ist durch Bakterien verursacht worden.	*The epidemic was caused by bacteria.*
Intermediary:	Die Familie wird durch einen Polizisten benachrichtigt.	*The family is informed by a police officer.*

Übung 16·7

Complete and rewrite each of the following incomplete sentences in three different ways.

1. Der Manager wird von ... entlassen werden.

   a. _____

   b. _____

   c. _____

2. Die alten Häuser sind durch ... zerstört worden.

   a. _____

   b. _____

   c. _____

Modal auxiliaries

Modal auxiliaries are most commonly used together with another verb in infinitive form: **er kann singen** (*he can sing*); **er muss singen** (*he must sing*). Modals are used in the same way with a "passive infinitive." A passive infinitive is composed of a past participle followed by the infinitive **werden: besucht werden** (*to be visited*); **gesehen werden** (*to be seen*).

When writing sentences with a modal auxiliary and an infinitive or passive infinitive, it is the modal auxiliary that is conjugated. That means that in the perfect tenses, the auxiliary will be **haben** and not **sein**, since all modal auxiliaries require **haben** as their auxiliary. First let's look at a passive sentence that is introduced by a variety of modal auxiliaries:

modal + participle + werden
Es kann + nicht veröffentlicht + werden.
It can't be published.

modal + participle + werden
Es muss + nicht veröffentlicht + werden.
It doesn't have to be published.

modal + participle + werden

Es soll + nicht veröffentlicht + werden.
It should not be published.

Now consider these examples of a passive sentence with a modal auxiliary in the various tenses:

Es kann nicht gemacht werden.	*It can't be done.*
Es konnte nicht gemacht werden.	*It couldn't be done.*
Es hat nicht gemacht werden können.	*It couldn't be done.*
Es wird nicht gemacht werden können.	*It won't be able to be done.*

Notice that in the present perfect and the future tenses, just like with a single infinitive, a passive infinitive forms a double infinitive structure with the modal auxiliary:

gemacht werden (passive infinitive) + **können** (modal infinitive)
→ **gemacht werden können**

Übung
16·8

Using the modal auxiliary in parentheses as your cue, rewrite the passive sentence provided in the present tense. Then rewrite the sentence in the present perfect tense.

EXAMPLE: (können) Es wird von Herrn Bauer repariert.

a. Es kann von Herrn Bauer repariert werden.

b. Es hat von Herrn Bauer repariert werden können.

1. (müssen) Der Säugling wird von der Mutter gefüttert.

a. _____

b. _____

2. (wollen) Die Gäste werden nicht schnell bedient.

a. _____

b. _____

3. (sollen) Der Artikel wird von dem besten Reporter geschrieben.

a. _____

b. _____

4. (können) Das Brot wird nicht in einer halben Stunde gebacken.

a. _____

b. _____

Using the verbs provided, write original passive sentences.

EXAMPLE: können, reparieren

<u>Der alte Wagen konnte nicht richtig repariert werden.</u>

1. müssen, abholen

_____

2. sollen, unterrichten

_____

3. können, schreiben

_____

4. dürfen, schreiben

_____

5. müssen, mieten

_____

6. sollen, besuchen

_____

7. dürfen, ansprechen

_____

Another passive form

As mentioned earlier, there is a second type of passive. It consists of a conjugation of the verb **sein** and a past participle. This second passive offers the past participle as an adjective. The difference between **werden** in the passive and **sein** in the passive is perhaps more clearly illustrated in English. Consider the following pair of sentences in the present tense:

> *The old clock **is being repaired**.*
> *The old clock **is repaired**.*

The first sentence shows an action that is in progress. The second sentence describes the clock as already being in a state of repair—it is adjectival in nature. In German, the difference is marked by the use of the two different auxiliaries:

> Die alte Uhr wird repariert.
> Die alte Uhr ist repariert.

If the participle in the two example sentences above is replaced with a true adjective, only the second sentence, with **sein**, will make sense without changing its meaning. The sentence with **werden**, on the other hand, would lose its passive meaning, **werden** reverts to its meaning of *to* *become* or *get*, and the sentence may not make complete sense. Compare the following two sentences, using the true adjective **unbezahlbar**, with the previous examples using the participle **repariert**:

Die alte Uhr wird unbezahlbar.	*The old clock becomes priceless.*
Die alte Uhr ist unbezahlbar.	*The old clock is priceless.*

werden + past participle → **passive sentence**

sein + past participle acting as adjective → **adjective**

Übung
16·10

*Change the following sentences, which are now in the first type of passive using **werden**, to sentences of the second type, using **sein**. Retain the tense of the original sentence.*

1. Der verwundete Mann wurde gerettet.

   _____

2. Die Haustiere werden gefüttert.

   _____

3. Die unartigen Kinder werden bestraft.

   _____

4. Die schöne Tasse wurde leider zerbrochen.

   _____

*Now compose three original passive sentences, using **werden** in either the present or past tense, and then rewrite each of them in the passive using **sein**.*

5. _____

   _____

6. _____

   _____

7. _____

   _____

The subjunctive mood

The subjunctive mood is avoided in modern English by many English speakers, in many instances. But German is different. The subjunctive mood is still an important part of the language and needs to be carefully considered in order to write good German sentences.

Subjunctive conjugations

There are two basic conjugations in the German subjunctive: One is called *subjunctive I* or *the present subjunctive* and the other is called *subjunctive II* or *the past subjunctive*. The terms *subjunctive I* and *subjunctive II* will be used here.

The following conjugational endings are basic to both forms of the subjunctive:

ich	-e	wir	-en
du	-est	ihr	-et
er/sie/es	-e	Sie/sie	-en

But subjunctive I applies them to the stem of the infinitive, and subjunctive II applies them to a past tense form. Let's look at some examples:

Suchen (*to look for*) is a regular verb. The subjunctive I conjugation has only a slight difference from the indicative present tense conjugation. And subjunctive II is identical to the indicative past tense conjugation:

	SUBJUNCTIVE I	SUBJUNCTIVE II
ich	suche	suchte
du	suchest	suchtest
er	suche	suchte
wir	suchen	suchten
ihr	suchet	suchtet
sie	suchen	suchten

Laufen (*to run*) is an irregular verb. Both subjunctive I and II are different in some degree from the indicative conjugation:

	SUBJUNCTIVE I	SUBJUNCTIVE II
ich	laufe	liefe
du	laufest	liefest
er	laufe	liefe
wir	laufen	liefen
ihr	laufet	liefet
sie	laufen	liefen

Kommen (*to come*) is also an irregular verb. But its irregular past tense form (**kam**) has an umlaut vowel (**a, o, u**). When an irregular verb has an umlaut vowel, its subjunctive II forms will require an umlaut:

	SUBJUNCTIVE I	SUBJUNCTIVE II
ich	komme	käme
du	kommest	kämest
er	komme	käme
wir	kommen	kämen
ihr	kommet	kämet
sie	kommen	kämen

Kennen (*to know*) is an irregular verb that has a vowel change in the past tense and also has the past tense suffix **-te** (**kannte**). When this verb is conjugated in subjunctive II, the vowel change is avoided. This also occurs with other verbs in this category, such as **nennen** (*to name*) and **brennen** (*to burn*):

	SUBJUNCTIVE I	SUBJUNCTIVE II
ich	kenne	kennte
du	kennest	kenntest
er	kenne	kennte
wir	kennen	kennten
ihr	kennet	kenntet
sie	kennen	kennten

Denken (*to think*) is another irregular verb that has a vowel change in the past tense and also has the past tense suffix **-te** (**dachte**). When this verb is conjugated in subjunctive II, the vowel change is maintained and an umlaut is added. This also occurs with other verbs in this category, such as **bringen** (*to bring*) and **wissen** (*to know*):

	SUBJUNCTIVE I	SUBJUNCTIVE II
ich	denke	dächte
du	denkest	dächtest
er	denke	dächte
wir	denken	dächten
ihr	denket	dächtet
sie	denken	dächten

Modals and the umlaut

Müssen (*to have to*) and other modal auxiliaries that have an umlaut in the infinitive keep the umlaut in subjunctive II. Modals that do not have an umlaut in the infinitive, e.g., **wollen** (*to want*), do not have one in subjunctive II:

	MÜSSEN	WOLLEN
ich	müsse müsste	wolle wollte
du	müssest müsstest	wollest wolltest
er	müsse müsste	wolle wollte
wir	müssen müssten	wollen wollten
ihr	müsset müsstet	wollet wolltet
sie	müssen müssten	wollen wollten

The auxiliaries **sein** (*to be*), **haben** (*to have*), and **werden** (*shall, will*) play an important role in tense formation. Let's look at their subjunctive I and II conjugations:

	SEIN		HABEN		WERDEN	
ich	sei	wäre	habe	hätte	werde	würde
du	seiest	wärest	habest	hättest	werdest	würdest
er	sei	wäre	habe	hätte	werde	würde
wir	seien	wären	haben	hätten	werden	würden
ihr	seiet	wäret	habet	hättet	werdet	würdet
sie	seien	wären	haben	hätten	werden	würden

Indirect discourse

Indirect discourse is the retelling of what someone else has said or asked. In *spoken* German, there is a tendency to use a subjunctive II conjugation in indirect discourse:

Er sagte, dass Frau Schmidt krank wäre.	*He said that Ms. Schmidt was sick.*

But in *written* German, sentences in indirect discourse more frequently conjugate verbs in subjunctive I:

Er sagte, dass Frau Schmidt krank sei.	*He said that Ms. Schmidt was sick.*

This use of the subjunctive I and subjunctive II conjugations occurs with both *indirect discourse* and *indirect questions*. For example:

Der Redner sagte, dass der globale Temperaturanstieg noch ein Problem sei.	*The speaker said that global warming was still a problem.*
Die Zeitung berichtete, dass der Präsident nach Berlin fliegen werde.	*The newspaper reported that the president would fly to Berlin.*
Herr Benz fragte, ob ihre Mannschaft gewonnen habe.	*Mr. Benz asked whether their team had won.*

sagen + **dass** + subjunctive I verb → indirect discourse

fragen + **ob** + subjunctive I verb → indirect question

When the subjunctive I conjugation is identical to the indicative present tense (for the verb **haben**, for instance, where the subjunctive I, **wir haben**, is identical to the indicative, **wir haben**), use the subjunctive II conjugation (**wir hätten**) in place of the subjunctive I conjugation. For example:

Karl erzählte, dass die Kinder im Garten (spielen) spielten.	*Karl said that the children were playing in the garden.*
Sie fragte, ob sie genug Geld (haben) hätten.	*She asked whether they had enough money.*

Use **ob** (*whether, if*) to introduce indirect discourse questions that can be answered with **ja** or **nein**:

Kann er verstehen? (Ja, er kann verstehen.)	*Can he understand? (Yes, he can understand.)*
Erik fragte, ob er verstehen könne.	*Erik asked whether he could understand.*

If a question is posed using an interrogative word, that interrogative word becomes the conjunction in indirect discourse and a subjunctive I conjugation is required. For example:

Wo wohnt er jetzt?

Er fragte, wo er jetzt wohne. — *He asked where he was living now.*

Warum ist sie wieder krank geworden?

Er fragte, warum sie wieder krank — *He asked why she had gotten sick again.*
geworden sei.

Wie viel Geld brauchen sie?

Er fragte, wie viel Geld sie brauchten. — *He asked how much money they needed.*

It is important to consider the tense of a verb in direct discourse. The past tense form of the subjunctive I conjugation in indirect discourse is not identical to the indicative past tense form. For example:

Present tense:	„Er singt sehr gut."
Indirect discourse:	Sabine sagte, dass er sehr *Sabine said that he sings very well.* gut singe.
Past tense:	„Er sang sehr gut."

or

Present perfect tense:	„Er hat sehr gut gesungen."
Indirect discourse:	Sabine sagte, dass er sehr *Sabine said that he had sung* gut gesungen habe. *very well.*
Future tense:	„Er wird sehr gut singen."
Indirect discourse:	Sabine sagte, dass er sehr *Sabine said that he would sing* gut singen werde. *very well.*

Direct discourse verbs in the past or perfect tenses are formed like present perfect conjugations when they are reported in indirect discourse:

er sang	→	er habe gesungen
er hat gesungen	→	er habe gesungen
er reiste	→	er sei gereist
er ist gereist	→	er sei gereist

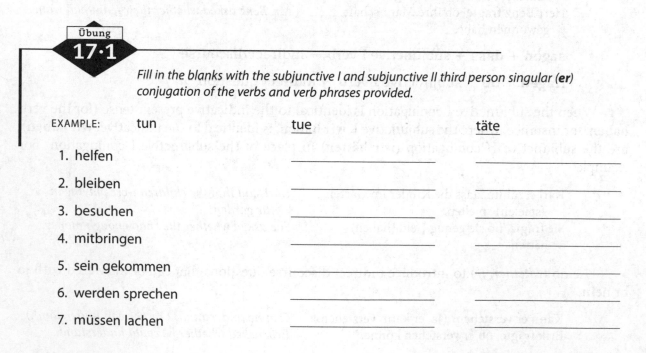

Übung

17·1

*Fill in the blanks with the subjunctive I and subjunctive II third person singular (**er**) conjugation of the verbs and verb phrases provided.*

EXAMPLE: tun <u>tue</u> <u>täte</u>

1. helfen _____ _____

2. bleiben _____ _____

3. besuchen _____ _____

4. mitbringen _____ _____

5. sein gekommen _____ _____

6. werden sprechen _____ _____

7. müssen lachen _____ _____

8. essen _____ _____

9. nennen _____ _____

10. werden gefunden werden _____ _____

Complete each line of indirect discourse with four original phrases, using the verbal signals given.

EXAMPLE: Er sagte, dass _____.

kaufen <u>Er sagte, dass er einen neuen Wagen gekauft habe.</u>

1. Der Reporter berichtete, dass _____.

a. küssen _____

b. stehlen _____

c. regieren _____

d. bleiben _____

2. Professor Benz fragte, ob _____.

a. schreiben _____

b. finden _____

c. sich benehmen _____

d. zerstören _____

3. Sie teilte mit, dass _____.

a. werden bestraft _____

b. müssen verteidigen _____

c. können bauen _____

d. haben gesehen _____

4. Frau Kamps erzählte, dass _____.

a. imponieren _____

b. ausgeben _____

c. verbessern _____

d. angreifen _____

Als ob, als wenn

The subjunctive II conjugation has another function besides being the preferred conjugation in German conversational indirect discourse. It is also used after the conjunctions **als ob** and **als wenn** (*as if*) and is an important element of writing good sentences:

Martin tut so, als ob er alles wüsste.
Sie spricht, als wenn ich ein dummes
    Kind wäre.

Martin acts as if he knew everything.
She speaks as if I were a stupid child.

With the conjunctions **als ob** and **als wenn**, just as with other subordinating conjunctions such as **dass** and **ob**, the conjugated verb in the subordinating clause is the final element.

Übung
17·3

Complete each sentence three times, each time introducing a subordinating clause with
als ob.

EXAMPLE: a. Der Torwart spielte, <u>als ob er krank wäre.</u>

b. Der Torwart spielte, <u>als ob er nicht laufen könnte.</u>

c. Der Torwart spielte, <u>als ob das Tor schon verteidigt wäre.</u>

1. a. Meine Schwester tut so, _____.

   b. _____

   c. _____

2. a. Der alte Mann lacht, _____.

   b. _____

   c. _____

3. a. Die Kinder singen, _____.

   b. _____

   c. _____

4. a. Meine Mutter weinte, _____.

   b. _____

   c. _____

Wenn

The subordinating conjunction **wenn** (*if*) also requires a verb with a subjunctive II conjugation in the clause that follows it. Again, since **wenn** is a subordinating conjunction, the verb in the subordinate clause will be the last element in the sentence.

Clauses that are introduced by **wenn** suggest a *wish* and can often stand alone without a main clause. The conjunction can be omitted from the sentence and presumed to be understood. In that case, the conjugated verb begins the sentence. For example:

Wenn wir nur mehr Geld hätten!	*If only we had more money!*
Hätten wir nur mehr Geld!	
Wenn er nicht so jung gestorben wäre!	*If he hadn't died so young!*
Wäre er nicht so jung gestorben!	
Wenn ich sie doch nicht verlassen hätte!	*If only I hadn't left her!*
Hätte ich sie doch nicht verlassen!	

Notice that the words **doch** and **nur** are often added to these sentences for emphasis.

Übung 17·4

*Use the information in the sentence provided to form a wish statement with **wenn**. Then rewrite the sentence, omitting **wenn**.*

EXAMPLE: Er ist nicht gesund.

a. <u>Wenn er doch gesund wäre!</u>

b. <u>Wäre er doch gesund!</u>

1. Ihr seid nicht bei mir.

a. _____

b. _____

2. Das Kind ist nicht fleißig.

a. _____

b. _____

3. Der arme Mann ist so unglücklich.

a. _____

b. _____

4. Ich kann ihnen nicht helfen.

a. _____

b. _____

5. Du hast so wenig Glück gehabt.

a. _____

b. _____

Subordinating clauses

Of course, you can also use a subordinate **wenn**-clause together with a main clause. In such cases, the **wenn**-clause sets a *condition* for the achievement of the action in the main clause: *If this condition existed, then this would occur.* In sentences of this type, a subjunctive II conjugation is used in both the **wenn**-clause and the main clause. When there is only one verb in the main clause, there is a tendency to use **würde** and an infinitive. For example, consider the following sentences with a condition set in the present:

Wenn es nicht so weit wäre, ginge ich zu Fuß dorthin. — *If it weren't so far, I'd go there on foot.*

Wenn es nicht so weit wäre, würde ich zu Fuß dorthin gehen.

Wenn wir genug Geld hätten, dann kauften wir ein neues Auto. — *If we had enough money, we'd buy a new car.*

Wenn wir genug Geld hätten, dann würden wir ein neues Auto kaufen.

wenn-clause with subjunctive II verb + main clause with subjunctive II verb

Wenn es nicht so weit wäre, + führen wir dorthin.
If it weren't so far, we'd drive there.

or

wenn-clause with subjunctive II verb + main clause with würde + infinitive

Wenn es nicht so weit wäre, + würden wir dorthin + fahren.
If it weren't so far, we'd drive there.

If the main clause has more than one verb form in it, such as a modal and an infinitive, **würde** is not used:

Wenn sie hier wäre, könnte sie uns helfen. — *If she were here, she could help us.*

Wenn er älter wäre, müsste er nicht zur Schule gehen. — *If he were older, he wouldn't have to go to school.*

The emphasis of sentences such as these can be shifted by changing the positions of the **wenn**-clause and the main clause:

Wenn sie uns nicht um Hilfe bäte, könnten wir ihr nicht helfen. — *If she wouldn't ask us for help, we couldn't help her.*

Wir könnten ihr nicht helfen, wenn sie uns nicht um Hilfe bäte. — *We couldn't help her if she wouldn't ask us for help.*

Übung
17·5

Complete each sentence by setting a condition in the present.

EXAMPLE: <u>Wenn ich mehr Zeit hätte</u>, würde ich meiner Mutter helfen.

1. _____, würden wir in die Stadt fahren.

2. _____, könnten die Jungen im Garten spielen.

3. _____, würde ich in Hamburg übernachten.

4. _____, würde sie aufhören zu weinen.

Now complete each sentence by providing the main clause of the sentence.

5. Wenn Erik reicher wäre, _____.

6. Wenn Onkel Hans das Klavier spielen könnte, _____.

7. Wenn Frau Benz ihn kennte, _____.

8. Wenn sie auf dem Balkon stünden, _____.

It is possible to form sentences such as these with the condition set in the past. This requires a verb structure consisting of **haben** or **sein** plus a past participle. Since there is more than one verb form in the structure, **würde** is not used:

<table>
<tr><td>Wenn es nicht so weit gewesen wäre,
    wären wir zu Fuß dorthin gegangen.</td><td>*If it hadn't been so far, we would have gone
    there on foot.*</td></tr>
<tr><td>Wenn wir genug Geld gehabt hätten,
    dann hätten wir ein neues Auto gekauft.</td><td>*If we had had enough money, we would have
    bought a new car.*</td></tr>
</table>

Übung
17·6

Complete each sentence by setting a condition in the past.

EXAMPLE: <u>Wenn ich mehr Zeit gehabt hätte</u>, hätte ich meiner Mutter geholfen.

1. _____, wären wir nach München gefahren.

2. _____, hätte er länger bleiben können.

3. _____, wäre das Kind schneller gesund geworden.

4. _____, hätte ich ihre Rede verstanden.

Now complete each sentence by providing the main clause of the sentence.

5. Wenn Sonja nicht krank gewesen wäre, _____.

6. Wenn das Wetter besser geworden wäre, _____.

7. Wenn ich einen neuen Laptop gekauft hätte, _____.

8. Wenn das Baby hätte schlafen können, _____.

Using the verb cues provided, write original sentences in the conditional. If the verb cues are infinitives, form the condition in the present. If the verb cues are provided with an auxiliary and participle, form the condition in the past.

EXAMPLE: tanzen / sich freuen

Wenn Andrea mit mir tanzte, würde ich mich sehr freuen.

haben getanzt / haben sich gefreut

Wenn Andrea mit mir getanzt hätte, hätte ich mich sehr gefreut.

1. kommen / sein

_____

2. sein gekommen / sein gewesen

_____

3. haben geholfen / sein gewesen

_____

4. haben gewusst / haben gefragt

_____

5. sein / machen

_____

6. sein / sein

_____

7. haben / haben

_____

8. sein gefahren / haben bleiben müssen

_____

9. sein gewesen / sein gegangen

_____

10. sein / schwimmen gehen

_____

Form sentences with a condition set in the present, using the subject cues provided.

EXAMPLE: Erik / Tina
            Wenn Erik mehr Geld hätte, würde er mit Tina ausgehen.

1. der Polizist / der Taschendieb

   _____

2. ihre Cousine / Sabine und Renate

   _____

3. die Kellnerin / die Gäste

   _____

4. der Sauerbraten / die Köchin

   _____

Punctuation

German uses the same punctuation marks as English, but in some cases they are used in a slightly different way. In order to write accurate sentences in German, you should be aware of those differences.

The period

The period is used to end a declarative sentence. The sentence must contain a subject and a predicate and make appropriate sense. In addition, any tense, voice, or mood can be used in a declarative sentence. When these conditions are met, you have a sentence, and the conclusion of that sentence is indicated by a period:

Onkel Franz hat in Bonn gewohnt.	*Uncle Franz lived in Bonn.*
Die Jungen laufen ins Wohnzimmer.	*The boys run into the living room.*
Die beiden Brüder wurden verhaftet.	*The two brothers were arrested.*

If a declarative sentence is composed of more than one clause, it still ends with a period. This is true whether the sentence contains dependent or independent clauses:

Der Lehrer, den die Schüler lieben, wurde entlassen.	*The teacher that the students love was fired.*
Wenn das Wetter besser wäre, würden wir spazieren gehen.	*If the weather were better, we'd go for a stroll.*
Ich weiß nicht, ob sie zu Hause ist.	*I don't know whether she's at home.*

The period has yet another function in writing: It is used to separate hours from minutes when giving the time and to identify a number that is used as an ordinal number in a date. When telling time, for the A.M. hours, you will write:

0.30 (null Uhr dreißig)	*12:30 A.M.*
6.15 (sechs Uhr fünfzehn/ Viertel nach sechs)	*6:15 A.M.*

For the P.M. hours, you will write:

15.25 (fünfzehn Uhr fünfunddreißig)	*3:15 P.M.*
24.00 (vierundzwanzig Uhr)	*12:00 midnight*

145

When giving dates, you will write:

der 3. März (dritte)	*the third of March/March third*
der 31. Oktober (einunddreißigste)	*the thirty-first of October/October thirty-first*
am 4. Juli (vierten)	*on the fourth of July/on July fourth*
am 19. Januar (neunzehnten)	*on the nineteenth of January/on January nineteenth*

The question mark

A question mark ends a sentence that asks for information. The question can be a yes-no question or a question that is introduced by an interrogative word. Questions can occur in any tense or voice:

Hat sie einen Preis gewonnen?	*Did she win a prize?*
Ist das bunte Hemd noch nicht verkauft worden?	*Hasn't the colorful shirt been sold yet?*
Wohin werdet ihr reisen?	*Where will you travel?*
Warum ist er im Einkaufszentrum geblieben?	*Why did he stay at the mall?*

Übung
18·1

Fill in the blanks with the missing word and punctuation mark: a period or a question mark.

EXAMPLE: Der starke Mann <u>hat</u> schwer gearbeitet <u>.</u>

1. _____ kommt der nächste Zug _____

2. _____ sie es verstünde, würde sie keine Fragen haben _____

3. _____ deine Tante wieder krank geworden _____

4. _____ sie keine Kinder _____

5. _____ die Ostsee rauher als die Nordsee _____

6. Die Kunden gehen in den Laden und _____ was sie brauchen _____

7. Hing ein Schild _____ der Tür des Ladens _____

8. _____ steht in der Ecke im Wohnzimmer _____

9. Mein _____ ist am 6 _____ April geboren.

10. _____ der Inter-City schneller als der Eilzug _____

Using the cues provided, write original declarative sentences that end with a period.

EXAMPLE: glauben / dass

Ich glaube es nicht, dass du wieder gelogen hast.

1. vergessen / dass

_____

2. sich interessieren / für

_____

3. sich freuen / auf

_____

Follow the same directions but form yes-no questions that end in a question mark.

4. größer / als

_____

5. so schön / wie

_____

6. aufstehen / um

_____

7. sich unterhalten / über

_____

Follow the same directions but form questions that begin with an interrogative word and end with a question mark.

8. das Schiff / untergehen

_____

9. das Rotkäppchen / treffen

_____

10. die Ente / tauchen

_____

The comma

In German, the comma is used to delineate clauses within a sentence. Even if there are no conjunctions to separate the clauses, the commas are still used; the clauses are treated like a series that is separated by commas. For example:

Im Sommer trafen sie sich im Park, sie lasen Gedichte und Erzählungen, sie unterhielten sich über Musik und Kunst.	*In summer, they met in the park, they read poems and stories, they conversed about music and art.*

In English, such long clauses in a sentence tend to be separated by a semicolon, but in German, although a semicolon might be used, the comma is preferred.

When a coordinating conjunction is used to link a clause to a main clause, a comma is used to separate the units. This occurs with declarative sentences or questions:

Er machte mit seinen Freunden eine Ferienreise, aber nach vier Tagen wollte er schon nach Hause kommen.	*He took a vacation trip with friends, but after four days he wanted to come home.*
Müssen wir hier bleiben, oder können wir morgen wieder nach Hause gehen?	*Do we have to stay here, or can we go back home tomorrow?*
In diesem Roman findest du keine Wahrheit, sondern nur die Fantasie des Schriftstellers.	*You won't find any truth in this novel, but rather the fantasy of the author.*

In this last example, note that the subject and verb are not written but understood (**..., sondern** *du findest* **nur die Fantasie des Schriftstellers.**).

Clauses introduced by a subordinating conjunction are separated from the main clause by a comma. This occurs with declarative sentences and questions. Some subordinating conjunctions can introduce the sentence or follow the main clause:

Sie fragten, ob Tante Luise in die Stadt mitfahren wollte.	*They asked whether Aunt Luise wanted to come along to the city.*
Erik besuchte seine Freundin, als er in Basel war.	*Erik visited his girlfriend when he was in Basel.*
Sie weiß, dass er Unrecht hat.	*She knows that he is wrong.*

A clause introduced by **als** often begins the sentence:

Als wir in den Bergen wohnten, mussten wir gefährliche Schneestürme ertragen.	*When we lived in the mountains, we had to endure dangerous blizzards.*

In some cases, it is possible to omit the conjunction **dass**. The clause that follows is still separated from the main clause by a comma, but the position of the conjugated verb changes:

Der Mann behauptete, er habe den Diebstahl nicht gesehen.	*The man insisted he hadn't seen the theft.*
Er sagte, er kenne den Fremden überhaupt nicht.	*He said he didn't know the stranger at all.*

There is a tendency to avoid using a comma with the coordinating conjunctions **und** and **aber**. But a comma can be used in order to make the meaning of the sentence clear. The other coordinating conjunctions, however, always require the use of a comma.

Very much like English, German will use commas to separate an explanatory phrase from the rest of the sentence. For example:

Angela Merkel, Kanzlerin der Bundesrepublik, wird die USA besuchen.	*Angela Merkel, Chancellor of the Federal Republic, will visit the United States.*
Das kleine Mädchen, außer sich vor Angst, fing an zu schreien.	*The little girl, beside herself with fear, began to scream.*

Such explanatory phrases are easy to identify, in that they are in essence an elliptical form of a relative clause. The two previous sentences could have contained the following relative clauses: **Angela Merkel, die Kanzlerin der Bundesrepublik ist, ...** and **Das kleine Mädchen, das außer sich vor Angst war, ...** .

Interjections and exclamations are also separated from the rest of the sentence by commas. For example:

Ach, ist das nicht schön?	*Oh, isn't that beautiful?*
Mensch, war das ein Glück!	*Man, was that a stroke of luck!*

A comma is also used to separate an infinitive clause from the main clause. This is especially true with infinitive clauses that begin with **um**, **ohne**, and **anstatt**:

Ich wollte hier bleiben, um meinen Eltern zu helfen.	*I wanted to stay here in order to help my parents.*
Er ging nach Hause, ohne sich von uns zu verabschieden.	*He went home without saying good-bye to us.*
Sie kauft sich eine Bluse, anstatt ein Geschenk für ihre Schwester zu kaufen.	*She's buying herself a blouse instead of buying a present for her sister.*

Other infinitive clauses that use **zu** will not require a comma unless there is a matter of confusion to be avoided:

Sind Sie bereit(,) den jungen Kandidaten zu unterstützen?	*Are you prepared to support the young candidate?*
Er hat vor(,) etwas anderes zu tun.	*He plans on doing something else.*

In German, a comma functions in the same way as a period does in English to separate a number from a decimal amount in measurements or in currency usage. For example:

2,5 Meter (zwei Meter fünfzig)	*two point five meters*
10,75 Liter (zehn Liter fünfundsiebzig)	*ten point seventy-five liters*
€9,50 (neun Euro fünfzig [Cent])	*nine euros and fifty cents*
€100,10 (hundert Euro zehn Cent)	*a hundred euros and ten cents*

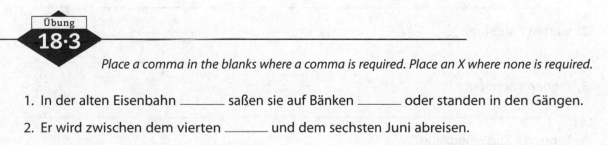

Übung

18·3

Place a comma in the blanks where a comma is required. Place an X where none is required.

1. In der alten Eisenbahn _____ saßen sie auf Bänken _____ oder standen in den Gängen.

2. Er wird zwischen dem vierten _____ und dem sechsten Juni abreisen.

3. Frau Keller _____ die Vorsitzende der Firma _____ war gar nicht zufrieden.

4. Die alte Dame _____ rot vor Erregung _____ konnte nicht sprechen.

5. Ich habe einen alten Schulkameraden angerufen _____ als ich in Oldenburg war.

6. Er lief an die Tür _____ um sie aufzumachen.

7. Der Professor _____ der sehr populär war _____ fragte _____ ob seine Studenten auf das Examen vorbereitet seien.

Übung 18·4

Complete each sentence in an appropriate way.

1. Professor Benz, _____, war sehr enttäuscht.

2. Als wir in Garmisch-Partenkirchen ankamen, _____.

3. Der Junge probierte den Kuchen, ohne _____.

4. Sie brachte _____, _____ und ihre Cousine mit.

5. Der Offizier ordnete an _____.

6. _____, außer sich vor Freude, _____.

7. Meine Verwandten sind gekommen, um _____.

Übung 18·5

Write original sentences that contain at least one comma. Include the cues provided in your sentences.

EXAMPLE: zu Hause / helfen

Wenn sie zu Hause wäre, würde sie ihrem Bruder helfen.

1. Gemüse / Obst

_____

2. warten / abfahren

_____

3. regnen / sondern

_____

4. Fahrrad / Zug / Flugzeug

_____

5. Esel / Pferd

_____

6. lesen / oder

_____

7. glauben / dass

_____

The colon

Just as is done in English, German uses a colon to introduce a concept or idea and to introduce a list of things. For example:

Einstein hatte die Welt mit einem neuen Begriff erstaunt: seine Relativitätstheorie.

Einstein astounded the world with a new concept: his theory of relativity.

Unter seinen beliebtesten Werken sind: die fünfte und die neunte Sinfonien.

Among his most beloved works are: the fifth and the ninth symphonies.

A colon is also used to introduce direct speech or discourse:

Plötzlich sagte Martin: „Ich liebe dich nicht mehr.“

Suddenly Martin said, "I don't love you anymore."

Dann fragte sie ihn: „Liebst du eine andere?“

Then she asked him, "Do you love someone else?"

Quotation marks

Perhaps you noticed in the previous two examples that the initial German quotation marks are located on the line, and the final quotation marks are located above:

above the line
„Ich liebe dich nicht mehr.“

"I don't love you anymore."

on the line

This also occurs when a single quotation mark is required inside another quoted phrase. For example:

Dann sagte er: „Ich habe ‚Buddenbrooks‘ nie gelesen.“

Then he said, "I've never read Buddenbrooks.*"*

The semicolon

Semicolons are used only rarely in German. Where you might use a semicolon in English, in German a comma is preferred. But there are instances when a writer would use a semicolon in order to indicate a pause greater than what a comma would imply:

In Bonn kann man mit einem Fahrschein der Straßenbahn einmal umsteigen; in Berlin kann man mehr als einmal umsteigen.

In Bonn you can make one streetcar transfer on one ticket; in Berlin you can transfer more than once.

The exclamation point

Naturally, an exclamation point is used to identify a sentence stated with great emotion or power. It is also the punctuation mark of greetings:

Das ist entsetzlich!	*That's horrible!*
Gott sei Dank!	*Thank God!*
Guten Tag!	*Good day. / Hello.*
Auf Wiedersehen!	*Good-bye.*

But the exclamation point is also the primary punctuation mark for imperative sentences. This is true whether the imperative is stated for the pronoun **du**, **ihr**, or **Sie**. The exclamation point is also used as the final element of a general imperative statement meant for a large group or as a public announcement:

Steh auf!	*Stand up. / Get up.*
Helft Tante Luise damit!	*Help Aunt Luise with that.*
Bitte schließen Sie sich hier an!	*Please line up here.*
Zurückbleiben!	*Stand back.*
Nicht rauchen!	*No smoking.*

Übung
18·6

Fill in the blanks in each sentence with the appropriate punctuation marks.

1. Die Richterin sagte zu dem Angeklagten _____ _____ Sie müssen antworten _____

   wenn ich Sie frage _____

2. Seien Sie vernunftig _____

3. Vorsicht _____ Zutritt verboten _____

4. Die Klägerin behauptete _____ _____ Der Hausmakler hat mich betrogen _____ _____

5. Die bestehenden Gesetze müssen beachtet werden _____ vor allem müssen die Richter und Anwälte jedes Gesetz genau befolgen.

6. Die Krankenschwestern müssen _____ solange Ärzte da sind _____ nicht selbstständig

   _____ sondern nach deren Anweisung handeln _____

7. Reisen jetzt viele Menschen im Flugzeug _____ weil es schneller ist _____ oder weil es

   nicht mehr gefährlich ist _____

Letter writing

If you were to write a letter to someone in the German-speaking world and you used the format used in writing a letter in English, your letter would undoubtedly arrive at its destination and be understood. The German and English formats are quite similar. But to be precise and to conform to the style preferred by German speakers, you need to know how the German format differs.

The address

On an envelope, the first line of an address is the addressee's title, followed by his or her name. Remember that **Frau** is used for both married and unmarried women, since the title **Fräulein** (*Miss*) is no longer in use. The next line in the address of an envelope contains the street and number, and that is followed by the **Postleitzahl** (*zip code*) and the city. Note that **Straße** is often abbreviated as **Str.** and the title **Doktor** can be abbreviated as **Dr.**:

Herrn
Martin Keller
Buchwaldstr. 92
79301 Freiburg

Frau Professor
Inge Bauer
Königsallee 14
30890 Hannover

If you are writing from outside of a German-speaking country to an address in either Switzerland, Austria, or Germany, you need to add the letters **CH** for Switzerland, **A** for Austria, or **D** for Germany before the zip code, for example: **D-79301 Freiburg**.

In a business letter written to someone at a company, the word **Firma** (*company*) is followed on the next line by the name of the company. Use the abbreviation **z. H.** (**zu Händen**) as the equivalent of *attention* in English:

Firma
Altdorf AG
z. H. Herrn Martin Keller
Buchwaldstr. 92
79301 Freiburg

Firma
Karl Benz
Finanzabteilung (*finance department*)
Königsallee 14
30890 Hannover

On the envelope of a business letter it is common to skip a line between the street address and the line with the zip code and city.

The sender's address appears on the back of the envelope, preceded by the word **Absender** or the abbreviation **Abs**:

Abs.
L. Baumann
Kalckreuthweg 7
20412 Hamburg-Othmarschen

Using the information provided, write the appropriate envelope addresses.

1. Hauptstraße 11 / Dorothea Schäfer / Ludwigshafen / 67021

   a. _____

   b. _____

   c. _____

   d. _____

2. Klassen & Meyer / Hermann Fitz / Berlin / 17712 / Hochstraße 55

   a. _____

   b. _____

   c. _____

   d. _____

   e. _____

The body of a letter

In both an informal German letter and a German business letter, the sender often does not write his or her address at the top of the letter. In a letter written from a business, the letter would be written on letterhead paper, which would provide the sender's information in that way. And in terms of personal letters, many people have personalized stationery, which usually gives their address at the top of the sheet.

Whether or not the letter was written on letterhead, at the top right of an informal letter or a business letter you will find the sender's location (usually the city) written on the line with the date and separated from it by a comma:

> Bremen, den 7. 11. 2008

Remember that the order of the numbers in a date is day, then month, then year (**den 7. 11. 2008** / *the seventh of November*, 2008). It is common to use the abbreviation **d.** in place of the article **den**:

> Oldenburg, d. 22. 9. 2009

The salutation (**die Anrede**) comes next. In the case of a letter to a friend or relative, the word **Lieber/Liebe** (*dear*) is used with a first name, but unlike the English word *dear*, it cannot be used with a plural. Each person in the salutation is greeted individually. For example:

Lieber Thomas	*Dear Thomas*
Liebe Tina	*Dear Tina*
Lieber Thomas, liebe Tina	*Dear Thomas and Tina*

However, if no name is used, and close friends or relatives are being addressed as a group, it is possible to use **Meine Lieben** (*my dears*).

In the text of the letter, it used to be the custom to capitalize the informal pronouns for *you* (**du**, **dich**, **dein**, **ihr**, **euch**, and **euer**). This is no longer the case, but you will still occasionally see the capitalized forms in letters written by someone from an older generation or by someone not accepting of the new rules of writing (**die neue Rechtschreibung**).

There are three basic ways of closing an informal letter:

Herzliche Grüße	*Yours (truly)*
Mit herzlichen Grüßen	*Yours truly, Kind regards*
Alles Liebe	*With love, All my love*

It is common to follow these kinds of informal closings with **dein** or **deine** and your first name.

In a formal letter that is not necessarily a business letter, the salutation **Lieber/Liebe** can be used with the title and last name of the person to whom you are writing:

Lieber Herr Benz
Liebe Frau Schmidt

If you are writing to a company, its name and address appear at the top left of the page. Just below that address, you can add a brief statement that describes the purpose of your letter:

Verkehrsverein Köln e. V.
Bahnhofstr. 18
56011 Köln

Hotels in Köln

In this kind of business letter, a more formal salutation is required. Note that different adjective endings are needed for the masculine and feminine:

Sehr geehrter Herr Keller
Sehr geehrte Frau Professor
Sehr geehrter Herr Doktor Hauser (*academic*)
Sehr geehrte Frau Doktor (*physician*)

In the first example above, the last name of the party being addressed is included, because the only title used is **Herr**. But if the person holds an additional title (as in the second example), the title *and not the last name* is used in a formal salutation. There is, however, an exception: If the last name is included with the title **Doktor**, this implies that the *doctor* being addressed is an academic and not a physician. If the party being addressed is a physician, the doctor's name is not included.

It is possible to use the formal salutation with a plural:

Sehr geehrte Damen und Herren	*Dear Sir or Madam / Ladies and Gentlemen*

In formal letters, the pronoun for *you* is **Sie**, and its forms are always capitalized in the text of the letter (**Ihnen** and **Ihr**). There are three commonly used closings for a formal letter:

Mit freundlichen Grüßen	*Yours sincerely, Yours truly*
Mit freundlichen Empfehlungen	*With kind regards, Yours faithfully*
Hochachtungsvoll	*Yours faithfully* (very formal)

It is common to place **Ihr** or **Ihre** (*yours*) after the closing line and just before your name, but that is an option:

Mit freundlichen Grüßen
Ihr
Thomas Keller

Mit freundlichen Grüßen
Ihre
Sabine Schneider

Whether writing an informal or a formal letter, there are two ways of punctuating the salutation: with a *comma* or with an *exclamation point*. If you use a comma, the first line of your letter will begin with a word that starts with a small letter, because the salutation is considered to be part of the sentence that follows it:

Lieber Rolf,	*Dear Rolf,*
es tut mir Leid, dass ich so lange gewartet	*I'm sorry that I've waited so long to answer*
habe deinen Brief zu beantworten....	*your letter. . . .*

If you punctuate your salutation with an exclamation point, the first line of your letter will begin with a capital letter:

Lieber Rolf!	*Dear Rolf,*
Es tut mir Leid, dass ich so lange ...	*I'm sorry that I've waited so long . . .*

The modern way

Some new and rather trendy ways of opening and closing a letter have developed. You should be aware of them, but be careful to use them only when appropriate. If you are writing to a friend or relative, you can begin your letter with a casual salutation, such as:

Hallo Tina!	*Hi, Tina,*

The closing of the letter would then normally also be casual:

Liebe Grüße	*Best regards,*

This casual format can also be used with people whose relationship to you is more formal. For example:

Hallo Frau Keller!
...
Liebe Grüße

Even a formal or business letter can have a more up-to-date salutation and closing:

Guten Tag, Herr Schmidt,
...
Freundliche Grüße

And if you do not have a specific addressee, you can still use a more modern salutation and closing:

Guten Tag!
...
Freundliche Grüße

In letters that are typed, your signature will follow the closing of the letter. It is important to type your name after your signature, so that the recipient of your letter knows precisely who you are and doesn't have to decipher your signature. If you have a job title, that will follow your name:

Mit freundlichen Grüßen	*Yours sincerely,*
(Ihre Unterschrift)	*(your signature)*
Michael Jones, Diplom-Ingenieur	*Michael Jones, Professional Engineer*

In both informal and formal letters, Germans often add a postscript (**das P.S.**). Just as in an English-language letter, it follows the closing and provides some additional information that was not included in the body of the letter.

Übung
19·2

Using the information provided, write three lines that give the date of the letter, the salutation, and the closing.

1. Berlin / June 6, 2008 / Doctor Reinhard Kalb (*your dentist*)

    a. _____

    b. _____

    c. _____

2. Bremen / March 29, 2009 / Sonja Schäfer (*your girlfriend*)

    a. _____

    b. _____

    c. _____

E-mail

Using e-mail for communication is just as important in Europe and the rest of the world as it is in North America. In German, e-mail is called **die E-Mail** or **die elektronische Post**. Let's look at the vocabulary used to identify the parts of an e-mail:

an	*to*
anhängen	*to attach*
Ansicht	*view*
bearbeiten	*to revise*
Betreff	*subject*
Cc	*copy*
Datei	*data file*
einfügen	*to insert*
Entwurf	*draft*
Größe	*size*
Hilfe	*help*
MIME-Typ	*MIME type*
Name	*name*
PGP Unterschreiben	*secure sign-in*
PGP Verschlüsseln	*encode for security*
senden	*to send*
später senden	*to send later*
Unterschrift	*signature*
von	*from*
Werkzeug	*tools*

E-mail addresses and websites have endings that identify the country in which the address or site is located. If it ends in **.de**, the country is Germany. If it ends in **.at**, the country is Austria. And if it ends in **.ch**, the country is Switzerland:

www.abendblatt.de
kundendienst@abc.at
www.basel.ch

Übung
19·3

Write a letter to a friend in Bremen thanking him or her for a birthday gift.

_____

_____

_____

_____

_____

_____

_____

Übung
19·4

Write a letter to a hotel in Munich to reserve a room.

_____

_____

_____

_____

_____

_____

_____

Write an e-mail message to a friend asking for help in finding a birthday gift.

_____

_____

_____

_____

_____

_____

_____

Let's write!

Übung
20·1

Using the string of words and phrases given, write an original sentence. Add any necessary words and conform to the grammar cues provided.

EXAMPLE: (*present perfect tense*) er / vergessen / weil / Mutter / krank / Krankenhaus

Er hat seinen Regenschirm vergessen, weil seine Mutter krank geworden ist und er sich zum Krankenhaus beeilt hat.

1. (*present perfect tense*) Freundin / freuen / Blumenstrauß / Geburtstag

_____

2. (*passive*) Zollbeamter / entlassen / weil / betrunken / spät

_____

3. (*past tense*) als / in der Hauptstadt / interviewen / Abgeordnete / fotografieren

_____

4. (*subjunctive II*) Schweden / reisen / wenn / kaltes Wetter / ertragen

_____

5. (*future tense*) ehemalige Freundin / neue Freundin / treffen / Hochzeitsfeier

_____

6. (*passive*) vor / Woche / Scheune / zerstören / durch

_____

7. (*present perfect tense*) sich benehmen / als ob / Preis / gewinnen

_____

Complete the following sentences with any appropriate phrase. Include the cue word or phrase in parentheses in your sentence.

1. Der Reporter berichtete, dass _____. (Friedensvertrag)

2. Ich will am Wochenende _____. (Fahrt nach)

3. Am Schalter lösen wir die Fahrkarten _____. (warten auf)

4. Sie steckte das Geld in ihre Tasche, weil _____. (verlieren)

5. Tina schreibt Briefe an ihre Familie in der Heimat _____. (dann)

6. Um wie viel Uhr _____? (anfangen)

7. Wenn ich ihn besser kennen würde, _____. (einladen)

8. Wie viel Grad _____? (im Schatten)

9. Martin ist um sechs aufgestanden, um _____. (füttern)

10. Die Kühe und Schweine wurden _____. (von)

11. _____, als wir Onkel Peter in Bonn besuchten. (Gewitter)

12. In _____ gründeten sie eine neue Stadt. (entfernt)

13. Der Professor wird _____ zeigen. (und)

14. Die beiden Brüder streiten sich _____. (Hund und Katze)

Fill in each blank with an appropriate adjective. Then rewrite the sentence, changing at least three elements in it but not the adjective(s) you have added.

EXAMPLE: Herr Schmidt besucht seinen kranken Onkel.

Angelika ruft ihren kranken Bruder an.

1. Die Eltern eines _____ Schülers sind sehr erfreut.

_____

2. Die _____ Touristen sind durch viele _____ Städte
gereist.

_____

3. Warum hat diese _____ Dame einen _____ Pelzmantel
kaufen wollen?

_____

4. Wird euer _____ Haus in dieser _____ Straße gebaut?

_____

5. Warum hat der _____ Mann dieser _____ Frau Geld geborgt?

_____

6. Sie behauptete, dass ihr _____ Sohn ganz _____ sei.

_____

7. Die Einwohner des _____ Dorfes freuten sich sehr über die

_____ Nachricht, dass der _____ Krieg endlich vorbei ist.

_____

8. Sie braucht ein paar _____ Straßenkleider, ein _____ Hauskleid und zwei _____ Pullover.

_____

9. Die reichlich _____ Apfelbäume beschenken uns _____ Herbst mit den _____ Äpfeln.

_____

10. In dem _____ Park gibt es mehrere _____ Seen und eine _____ Zahl _____ Spaziergänge.

_____

Form complete sentences using the cues given and any phrases that are appropriate for completing the sentence. Use the tense provided in parentheses.

EXAMPLE: (past) Ihre Tochter war klug, aber ihr Sohn war ziemlich dumm.

1. (present) _____ ebenso

teuer _____.

2. (past) _____ viel schärfer _____.

3. (future) _____ weiter

springen _____.

4. (past) _____ am längsten.

5. (present perfect) _____ eine viel

hübschere _____.

6. (*present*) _____ der kürzeste

Weg _____?

7. (*future*) _____ nicht

billiger _____.

8. (*present perfect*) _____ vollendet,

oder _____?

9. (*present*) _____ nicht

fleißiger _____.

10. (*past*) _____ der tiefste.

Write five phrases that could be responses to the interrogative word provided. You do not have to write complete sentences.

EXAMPLE: Wer?

ein paar Freunde von mir

seine Geschwister

die neulich gewählte Kanzlerin

Ihre beiden Schwägerinnen

alle Wissenschaftler der Welt

1. Was?

a. _____

b. _____

c. _____

d. _____

e. _____

2. Warum?

a. _____

b. _____

c. _____

d. _____

e. _____

3. Wohin?

a. _____

b. _____

c. _____

d. _____

e. _____

4. Was für ein/eine?

a. _____

b. _____

c. _____

d. _____

e. _____

5. Welcher/Welche/Welches?

a. _____

b. _____

c. _____

d. _____

e. _____

6. Wie weit?

a. _____

b. _____

c. _____

d. _____

e. _____

7. Wie oft?

a. _____

b. _____

c. _____

d. _____

e. _____

Now it's time to write completely original sentences without conforming to a paradigm or in response to cues. The only suggestions you need to follow are the topics provided for your writing. Be sure to challenge yourself. Do not take the easy road, because if you've gotten this far in this book, you're ready for some real writing.

Übung
20·6

Write a paragraph describing the schools you attended, your favorite teachers and subjects, friends you made, activities you participated in, degrees you have earned, how you wish to apply your education to your career. Include the following structures in your paragraph: a. a comparative adverb, b. a superlative adverb, and c. a double infinitive with a modal auxiliary.

_____

_____

_____

_____

_____

_____

_____

Übung
20·7

*Write a paragraph that describes the plot of a book or the content of an article that you have recently read. Include the following structures in your paragraph: a. indirect discourse, b. the subjunctive with the conjunction **wenn**, and c. a possessive relative pronoun.*

_____

_____

_____

_____

_____

_____

_____

Choose one of the following titles and write a short story. Include the following structures in your paragraph: a. the conjunction **als ob**, b. the passive voice in the present perfect tense, and c. **möchte**.

Liebe auf dem ersten Blick

Der fröhliche Wanderer

Mein Computer lebt

Tod in Salzburg

Angriff der Außerirdischen

_____

_____

_____

_____

_____

_____

_____

_____

Answer key

1 Declarative sentences and word order

1·1   1. a. Martin sprach kein Englisch. b. Martin hat kein Englisch gesprochen. c. Martin wird kein Englisch sprechen. 2. a. Ich kann es machen. b. Ich konnte es machen. c. Ich habe es machen können. 3. a. Eine Schlange frisst den Frosch. b. Eine Schlange frass den Frosch. c. Eine Schlange wird den Frosch fressen. 4. a. Über dem Wald fliegen viele Vögel. b. Über dem Wald sind viele Vögel geflogen. c. Über dem Wald werden viele Vögel fliegen.

1·2   1. Das ist nicht das beste Buch. 2. Sie ist nicht am Nachmittag angekommen. 3. Ihr Mann ist nicht bei einem Unglück umgekommen. 4. Er hat nicht helfen wollen. 5. Frau Schneider hat sich nicht wohl gefühlt. 6. Die Studenten sitzen nicht im Lesesaal. 7. Seine Frau hat ihn nicht betrogen.

1·3   1. Meine Großmutter trinkt keinen Kaffee. 2. Boris hat keine interessanten Bücher gefunden. 3. Die Jungen haben keinen Kindern geholfen. 4. Der Dieb hat kein Wort gesagt. 5. In diesem Wald gibt es keine Bären. 6. Ich werde das unter keinen Umständen tun.

1·4   1. Ihr Sohn hat nicht mitgehen wollen. 2. Die Leute gehen nicht in seinen Laden. 3. Ich klebte die Marke nicht auf den Brief. 4. Der Bodensee ist nicht der größte See. 5. Kein Mann spricht mit ihm. 6. Die Lehrerin brauchte keinen Kugelschreiber. 7. Der betrunkene Mann fährt nicht schnell.

1·5   1. Niemand will Schlittschuh laufen. 2. Der Polizist wird niemanden verhaften. 3. Manfred geht niemals in die Stadt. 4. Meine Verwandten waren nie in Berlin. 5. Sonja wird niemanden in Hamburg besuchen. 6. Er will nichts zu essen haben.

1·6   1. Leider ist sie wieder krank geworden. 2. Den ganzen Tag blieb Martin zu Hause. 3. Meine Freizeit verbringe ich in der Bibliothek. 4. Als ich um die Ecke kam, begegnete ich meinen Nachbarn. 5. Im Herbst möchte ich nach Italien reisen. 6. Wenn sie in London ist, geht sie oft ins Theater.

1·7   1. Den Wecker hat er reparieren lassen. 2. Das wissen sie nicht. 3. Schach spielen die Jungen. 4. Das muss man nicht. 5. Einen Mantel kaufte die Frau im Kaufhaus.

1·8   *Sample answers are provided.* 1. a. Oft isst meine Familie italienisch. b. Am Wochenende isst meine Familie italienisch. c. Wenn Onkel Otto uns besucht, isst meine Familie italienisch. 2. a. Gestern spielte Sonja Tennis. b. Nach der Schule spielte Sonja Tennis. c. Nachdem sie von der Schule kam, spielte Sonja Tennis. 3. a. Jetzt wird seine Freundin einen neuen Wagen kaufen. b. Im Februar wird seine Freundin einen neuen Wagen kaufen. c. Bevor sie abfährt, wird seine Freundin einen neuen Wagen kaufen.

1·9   1. In einer Woche werden wir wieder in Wien sein. 2. Meine Mutter musste um sechs Uhr aufstehen und in die Stadt fahren. 3. Als ich in der Hauptstadt war, ging ich oft ins Museum.

1·10   *Sample answers are provided.* 1. Jemand steht an der Tür und klopft. 2. Vor einer Woche kaufte mein Vater einen gebrauchten Wagen. 3. Um zehn Uhr begann die Vorstellung.

2 Interrogative sentences

2·1   1. Ist sein Vetter in der Hauptstadt gewesen?   2. Will Gudrun die Wahrheit über das Unglück erfahren?   3. Litt die kranke Frau an einer Vergiftung?   4. Muss man alle Verkehrszeichen beachten?   5. Durfte ich Luise und Tanja begleiten?   6. Ist etwas in der Küche los?   7. Freute sich meine Tante auf das Wiedersehen mit ihren Verwandten?

2·2   1. Spielen Sie Schach?   2. Musst du heute zu Hause bleiben?   3. Bist du noch nicht zur Arbeit gegangen?   4. Werden sie um zehn Uhr ankommen?

2·3   1. Für wen hatte Maria ein Geschenk?   2. Mit wem möchte Peter tanzen?   3. Wem wollen die Verwandten in Deutschland helfen?   4. Wessen Kinder werden mit Liebe erzogen?   5. Wen möchten sie morgen besuchen?

2·4   1. Was habe ich im Schaufenster gesehen?   2. Wem wird der Gerber das Fell abziehen?   3. Was ziehen die Bauern auf?   4. Wessen Nase war sehr kalt?

2·5   1. Wofür interessiert sich Herr Bauer?   2. Worauf will ich nicht länger warten?   3. Wovon hat der Lehrling nicht gehört?   4. Wonach sehnen sich die neuen Auswanderer?   5. Womit spielten die Kinder?   6. Worum habe ich meine Freunde gebeten?   7. Wogegen kämpfte der Professor?

2·6   1. Wie sprach der Rechtsanwalt?   2. Was für einen Pullover hat die junge Dame gekauft?   3. Warum muss ich einen Mantel tragen?   4. Welcher Junge ist ziemlich dumm?   5. Wo studiert seine Tochter?

2·7   1. Wie groß ist unser Schlafzimmer?   2. Wie viele Nelken hat Onkel Peter gekauft?   3. Wie alt wird Doktor Schmidt am elften Dezember werden?

2·8   *Sample answers are provided.*   1. Was fiel von dem Dach auf die Straße?   2. Klettert der Bergsteiger den steilen Felsen hinauf?   3. Mit wem hast du so lange getanzt?   4. Wie lange müsst ihr in der Hauptstadt auf euren Zug warten?   5. Kannst du mich zum Bahnhof begleiten?   6. Welches Geschäft hat die besten Preise?   7. Wodurch schützt man die Pflanzen vor der Kälte des Winters?

2·9   *Sample answers are provided.*   1. Was für ein Geschenk haben Sie gekauft?   2. Auf wen wartet ihr so lange?   3. Worauf freuen sich die Schüler?   4. Wohin reisen deine Eltern im Sommer?

3 Questions and answers

3·1   1. a. Wessen Lehrer wird nach Irak fahren? b. Wohin wird unser Lehrer fahren?   2. a. Was verbindet die Nordsee mit der Ostsee? b. Womit verbindet der Kieler Kanal die Nordsee?   3. a. Was bringen sie zum Tierarzt? b. Zu wem (Wohin) bringen sie den Kanarienvogel?   4. a. Welches Wörterbuch kostet vierzig Euro? b. Wie viel kostet das große Wörterbuch?   5. a. Trägt der alte Herr immer einen alten Hut? b. Was für einen Hut trägt der alte Herr?   6. a. In wessen Hauptstraßen gibt es viele interessante Geschäfte? b. Wie viele interessante Geschäfte gibt es in den Hauptstraßen einer Großstadt?   7. a. Wen brachte der Polizist zum Polizeiamt? b. Wohin brachte der Polizist den verhafteten Dieb?

3·2   *Sample answers are provided.*   1. Ja, gute Sprachkenntnisse sind jedem Menschen nützlich.   2. Der Arzt machte dem Kranken große Hoffnungen.   3. Sie müssen die deutsche Sprache lernen, weil Deutsch in Deutschland, Österreich und in der Schweiz gesprochen wird.   4. Ich komme aus Deutschland.   5. Unser Vetter aus Amerika war letzten Sommer hier.   6. Der Student arbeitet fleißig.   7. Sie erfuhr das Unglück durch einen Brief.   8. Der Vater soll für seine Kinder sorgen.   9. Die Mutter liebt ihre Kinder am meisten.   10. Man trinkt Tee oder Kaffee aus einer Tasse.

3·3   1. Was müssen sich die Kinder waschen?   2. Worüber kreiste ein weißer Storch?   3. Nach wem fragen die Gäste?   4. Auf wen mussten sie zwei Stunden warten?   5. In wen hat sich Wilhelm verliebt?   6. Was gelingt ihr nicht?   7. Wem muss er die Wolle scheren?   8. Wem kann ich nicht glauben?   9. Wessen Tod betrübt die Lehrerin?   10. Was freut uns?

3·4   *Sample answers are provided.*   1. Der Vater tadelt seinen Sohn.   2. Sie wollen eine Reise durch Italien machen.   3. Meine Mutter liebt es nicht, nach dem Essen zu rauchen.   4. Die Eltern freuten sich über die Geburt ihres Kindes.   5. Es ist nicht möglich so viel Geld zu sparen.   6. Diese Handschuhe gehören Herrn Schneider.   7. Herr Schäfer hat den Wagen seiner Tochter reparieren lassen.   8. Der Fahrer wird seinen kaputten Wagen auf die Straße schieben.   9. Wir fahren mit dem Zug ins Ausland.   10. Die arme Frau musste bei Verwandten wohnen.

3·5   1. Wie oft kommt er spät zur Schule?   2. Warum dürfen die Kinder nicht im Park spielen?   3. Mit wem hat meine Nichte einen Ausflug gemacht?   4. Was für ein Abendkleid trug die alte Dame?   5. Wie singt der süße kleine Junge?   6. Wem will der Fremdenführer die schönen Gemälde zeigen?   7. Wann ist ihr erster Sohn geboren?   8. Wie tanzt seine Tochter?   9. Wie spielt das Kind Geige?   10. Was darf man in diesem Restaurant nicht tun?

3·6   *Sample answers are provided.*   1. In der Kirche darf man nicht rauchen.   2. Du sollst deine Freunde am Bahnhof erwarten.   3. Der Mann liegt den ganzen Tag im Bett, weil er faul ist.   4. Ich soll einen gestreiften Schlips tragen.   5. Sie haben vom Tod ihres Großvaters durch die Zeitung erfahren.   6. Die Studentin interessiert sich für die Physik.   7. Diese Leute laufen zum Stadtpark.   8. Sie haben einen Pullover und eine Jacke gekauft.   9. Ihr Geburtstag ist am zweiten Januar.   10. Die weinenden Kinder suchen ihre Eltern.

3·7   *Sample answers are provided.*   1. a. Warum spielst du nicht mit den anderen Kindern? b. Ich spiele nicht mit den anderen Kindern, weil sie zu jung sind.   2. a. Woher hat er diese alten Bücher bekommen? b. Er hat diese alten Bücher von einem Freund bekommen.   3. a. Wie viel Meter Stoff hat Frau Benz gebraucht? b. Frau Benz hat vier Meter Stoff gebraucht.   4. a. Wie oft seid ihr ins Ausland gereist? b. Wir sind nur einmal ins Ausland gereist.

3·8   *Sample answers are provided.*   1. a. Wann musst du aufstehen? b. Ich muss morgen früh aufstehen.   2. a. Warum bleibt ihr zu Hause? b. Wir bleiben zu Hause, weil wir kein Geld haben.   3. a. Wie lange dauert der Film? b. Der Film dauert zwei Stunden.   4. a. Wohin wollen sie heute gehen? b. Sie wollen heute ins Kino gehen.

4   Imperatives

4·1   1. trink(e)!, trinkt!, trinken Sie!   2. stell(e) an!, stellt an!, stellen Sie an!   3. tu(e)!, tut!, tun Sie!   4. brich!, brecht!, brechen Sie!   5. empfiehl!, empfehlt!, empfehlen Sie!   6. fahr(e) ab!, fahrt ab!, fahren Sie ab!   7. lies!, lest!, lesen Sie!   8. nimm!, nehmt!, nehmen Sie!   9. iss!, esst!, essen Sie!   10. stiehl!, stehlt!, stehlen Sie!

4·2   *Sample answers are provided.*   1. Helft mir damit!   2. Essen Sie nicht in diesem Restaurant!   3. Schreiben Sie dem Rechtsanwalt einen Brief!   4. Besuchen Sie den neuen Patienten!   5. Sei artig!   6. Friss langsam!   7. Lade Sonja und Gudrun ein!   8. Werde gesund!   9. Antwortet schneller!   10. Steigen Sie in der Bismarckstraße aus!

4·3   *Sample answers are provided.*   1. Vorsicht! Zurückbleiben!   2. Bitte nicht anfassen!   3. Bitte von links anstellen!   4. An der nächsten Haltestelle aussteigen!

4·4   1. Segeln wir in den Hafen!   2. Steigen wir am Marktplatz ein!   3. Essen wir im Schnellimbiss!   4. Lesen wir die amerikanischen Zeitungen!   5. Fahren wir nicht um die Ecke!   6. Legen wir die Kinder aufs Bett!   7. Fragen wir einen Polizisten, wo die Bank ist!

4·5   1. a. Lass sie morgen ausschlafen! b. Lass uns morgen ausschlafen!   2. a. Lass ihn den letzten Apfel essen! b. Lass uns den letzten Apfel essen!   3. a. Lass ihn nicht im kalten Fluss schwimmen! b. Lass uns nicht im kalten Fluss schwimmen!   4. a. Lasst die Mädchen mit den Kindern spielen! b. Lasst uns mit den Kindern spielen!   5. a. Lasst ihn die neue Kunsthalle besuchen! b. Lasst uns die neue Kunsthalle besuchen!   6. a. Lassen Sie sie um achtzehn Uhr anfangen! b. Lassen Sie uns um achtzehn Uhr anfangen!   7. a. Lassen Sie Herrn Bauer in die Heimat zurückkehren! b. Lassen Sie uns in die Heimat zurückkehren!

4·6   *Sample answers are provided.*   1. Sprechen Sie bitte ein bisschen lauter!   2. Seid artig und sagt nichts!   3. Besucht uns nächste Woche!   4. Betet für mich!   5. Lasst uns im Garten spazieren gehen!   6. Lassen Sie mich in Ruhe!   7. Lassen Sie ihn zum Stadtpark gehen!

5   Coordinating conjunctions

5·1   1. Er wollte Tennis spielen, denn das Wetter war endlich gut.   2. Ich habe es nicht verloren, sondern habe es hinter dem Schrank versteckt.   3. Paul studiert in Berlin und wohnt in einem Studentenheim.   4. Sei ruhig, oder geh sofort nach Hause!   5. Soll er einen roten Wagen kaufen, oder soll er einen blauen Wagen kaufen?   6. Ich höre was du sagst, aber ich verstehe dich nicht.   7. Angela spielt Gitarre und ihr Bruder spielt Flöte.

5·2   *Sample answers are provided.*   1. Sie versuchte ihn zu warnen, aber seine Brieftasche fiel doch ins Wasser.   2. Die Studentin konnte nicht arbeiten, denn sie hörte die laute Musik.   3. Normalerweise ist der Herbst am schönsten, aber letztes Jahr war der Frühling schön.   4. Karl ist nicht zum Café gegangen, sondern hat eine alte Freundin besucht.   5. Der Schüler setzte sich auf seinen Platz und nahm seinen Bleistift in die Hand.   6. Im Schaufenster stehen große Puppen, aber niemand kauft sie.   7. Peter schreibt den Aufsatz nicht, sondern er sieht den ganzen Abend fern.   8. Herr Benz pflegt den Blumengarten und seine Frau pflegt den Gemüsegarten.   9. Ich habe kein Sprudelwasser gekauft, sondern nur ein paar Flaschen Bier. 10. Ich habe sein letztes Buch gelesen, aber ich habe ihm kein Wort geglaubt.

5·3   *Sample answers are provided.*   1. Tun Sie mir den Gefallen und kommen Sie mit!   2. Der Junge muss gehorchen, oder er hat die Folgen selbst zu tragen.   3. Die Kirschen schmecken sehr gut, aber wie viel kosten sie?   4. Wir machen keine Pause, sondern arbeiten bis spät in die Nacht.

5·4   *Sample answers are provided.*   1. Ich habe kein Geld, aber ich will eines Tages eine Europareise machen. 2. Die Bauern hoffen auf Regen, denn der Sommer ist wieder trocken.   3. Hast du genug Geld, oder bist du wieder pleite?   4. Sie reisen nicht nach Kanada, sondern nach Amerika.

6   Subordinating conjunctions

6·1   1. Wann legt er sich ins Bett?   2. Sie musste das Studium aufgeben, als ihr Vater starb.   3. Als ich die Universität verließ, traf ich einen Freund.   4. Man geht zum Arzt, wenn man krank ist.   5. Wann hat man Husten und Schnupfen?   6. Als er im letzten Jahr in Kiel war, begegnete er einem Schulkameraden. 7. Wenn die Kinder sechs Jahre alt sind, kommen sie in die Grundschule.

6·2   *Sample answers are provided.*   1. Wenn du nach Berlin reist, sollst du deinen Personalausweis bei dir haben.   2. Wenn Sie in Düsseldorf sind, dürfen Sie vorbeikommen.   3. Als die Touristen Südamerika besuchten, lernten sie ein paar spanische Wörter.   4. Herr Schneider trifft einen Bekannten, wenn er im Stadtpark sitzt.   5. Wenn du isst, sollst du nicht sprechen.   6. Wenn es anfängt zu schneien, denken die Kinder an Weihnachten.   7. Wenn du London besuchst, gehst du oft ins Theater?

6·3   *Sample answers are provided.*   1. Während wir im Ruhrgebiet waren, besuchten wir viele Fabriken. 2. Bevor Herr Bauer starb, schrieb er sein Testament.   3. Bevor wir abfahren, müssen wir die Koffer packen.   4. Obwohl sie meine Schwester war, wollte ich ihr kein Geld leihen.   5. Wissen Sie, ob das Rathaus weit ist?   6. Wir kommen morgen vorbei, falls wir genug Zeit haben.   7. Fahren wir zum Bahnhof mit einem Taxi, damit wir den Zug erreichen!   8. Soviel wir wissen, ist sie wieder schwanger. 9. Sie können mit uns reiten, sooft Sie wollen.   10. Ich kann nicht warten, bis er zurückkommt.   11. Ehe er zur Party ging, kämmte er sich wieder die Haare.   12. Ich habe ihnen geholfen, soviel ich konnte. 13. Da Lukas betrunken war, wollte sie nicht mit ihm tanzen.   14. Hast du gewusst, dass du den letzten Bus verpasst hast?

6·4   *Sample answers are provided.*   1. Obwohl ich gut zuhörte, verstand ich es nicht.   2. Während sie im Lager wohnten, haben sie oft Schach gespielt.   3. Er musste wieder zu Fuß gehen, weil er eine Panne hatte. 4. Erik fragte uns, ob wir ins Theater gehen wollen.   5. Sie haben nichts bezahlt, solange sie kein heißes Wasser hatten.   6. Kinder, wartet hier, bis die Ampel grün ist!   7. Ich habe keine Ahnung, wie die Dame aussieht.   8. Beeilt euch, damit wir den Bus nicht verpassen!   9. Da er müde war, wollte er nach Hause gehen.   10. Obwohl es kalt und sonnig ist, will ich nicht Skilaufen gehen.   11. Seitdem sie ihren Führerschein bekam, ist sie nie zu Hause.   12. Nachdem er sich den Finger verletzt hatte, fing er an zu heulen.   13. Wir wissen nicht, ob er uns versteht.   14. Du musst am Tisch bleiben, bis du das Glas Milch ausgetrunken hast.

6·5   1. Ich weiß nicht, wer in unserem Schwimmbad schwimmt.   2. Ich weiß nicht, ob das Mädchen das Geld verloren hat.   3. Ich weiß nicht, warum er dem alten Mann drohte.   4. Ich weiß nicht, ob er diese Probleme lösen kann.   5. Ich weiß nicht, wie alt sein Urgroßvater war.   6. Ich weiß nicht, wem der Sohn ähnlich ist.   7. Ich weiß nicht, wonach der kranke Herr fragte.   8. Ich weiß nicht, wie lange die Vorstellung dauern wird.   9. Ich weiß nicht, was sie ihren Gästen zeigt.   10. Ich weiß nicht, ob der Fotograf die Aufnahmen entwickelte.   11. Ich weiß nicht, woran die alte Dame gern denkt.   12. Ich weiß nicht, um wen er sich viele Sorgen macht.   13. Ich weiß nicht, um wie viel Uhr der Mann in sein Büro geht. 14. Ich weiß nicht, was der Fremdenführer den Touristen wird zeigen wollen.

6·6   *Sample answers are provided.*   1. Tina blieb in der Stadt, bis ihre Tante wieder gesund war.   2. Ich erzähle dir seine Geschichte, damit du ihn besser verstehst.   3. Während es donnerte und blitzte, saßen wir im kleinen Paddelboot.   4. Frau Benz kaufte die Bluse, obwohl der Preis sehr hoch war.   5. Das Kind war so müde, dass es sofort einschlief.   6. Seitdem das Wetter wieder schlecht wurde, mussten die Kinder im Keller spielen.   7. Wenn sie ihre Verwandten besuchen, sind sie am glücklichsten.

6·7   *Sample answers are provided.*   1. Wissen Sie, ob der Zug pünktlich ankommen wird?   2. Andreas kann nicht mitkommen, weil er pleite ist.   3. Ich erzählte ihm alles, damit er das Problem besser versteht. 4. Als es dunkel wurde, suchte sie in der Küche nach einer Kerze.

7 Relative pronouns

7·1 1. Die Frau, deren Tochter Köchin ist, wollte die Suppe nicht schmecken. 2. Er hilft seinen Verwandten, die in den Bergen wohnen. 3. Sie segelten zu einer Insel, die von keinen Menschen bewohnt wurde. 4. Es ist ein deutsches Flugzeug, das eben gelandet ist. 5. Der alte Herr, dessen Vermögen verloren ging, musste bei seinem Bruder wohnen. 6. Er trifft auf der Straße einen Freund, dessen Gesicht ganz blass ist. 7. Sie sieht die Soldaten, von denen das kleine Dorf besetzt wurde. 8. Die Universität, in deren Räumen eine Konferenz stattfindet, ist weltbekannt. 9. Der Mann, für den Tina gearbeitet hat, ist neulich gestorben. 10. Der Stuhl, auf dem Oma sitzt, ist alt und wackelig.

7·2 1. Die Frau, deren Tochter Köchin ist, wollte die Suppe nicht schmecken. 2. Er hilft seinen Verwandten, welche in den Bergen wohnen. 3. Sie segelten zu einer Insel, welche von keinen Menschen bewohnt wurde. 4. Es ist ein deutsches Flugzeug, welches eben gelandet ist. 5. Der alte Herr, dessen Vermögen verloren ging, musste bei seinem Bruder wohnen. 6. Er trifft auf der Straße einen Freund, dessen Gesicht ganz blass ist. 7. Sie sieht die Soldaten, von welchen das kleine Dorf besetzt wurde. 8. Die Universität, in deren Räumen eine Konferenz stattfindet, ist weltbekannt. 9. Der Mann, für welchen Tina gearbeitet hat, ist neulich gestorben. 10. Der Stuhl, auf welchem Oma sitzt, ist alt und wackelig.

7·3 *Sample answers are provided.* 1. a. Er lud seine Freunde, die auch an der Uni studieren, ein. b. Er lud seine Freunde, die er seit zehn Jahren kennt, ein. 2. a. Wer hat die Uhr, die wir so elegant finden, gekauft? b. Wer hat die Uhr, von der alle sprechen, gekauft? 3. a. Andreas spielte mit dem Hund, nach dem unser Nachbar fragte. b. Andreas spielte mit dem Hund, dessen Fell schneeweiß ist. 4. a. Alle respektieren die Richterin, gegen die der Bürgermeister sprach. b. Alle respektieren die Richterin, mit der sich der Kanzler treffen wird.

7·4 *Sample answers are provided.* 1. Wer andere Menschen hasst, den kann sie nicht lieben. 2. Wer zu oft lügt, dem glaube ich nicht. 3. Wem das Buch nicht gefällt, der soll es nicht lesen. 4. Wer nicht ehrlich ist, dem bleibt man fern. 5. Wer nicht für mich ist, der ist gegen mich. 6. Wem es nicht gefällt, der soll es nicht probieren. 7. Wer nicht gehorcht, der wird vom Vater verprügelt.

7·5 *Sample answers are provided.* 1. Ist das das Beste, was Sie zu verkaufen haben? 2. Der Kranke hat etwas gegessen, was er nicht hat vertragen können. 3. Sie haben eine gute Prüfung gemacht, was die Eltern sehr erfreute. 4. Haben Sie nichts, was billiger ist? 5. Leider gibt es vieles, worum sich niemand kümmert. 6. Sie sahen etwas, was unvergesslich war. 7. Der Reisende erzählte vieles, was das Publikum nicht verstehen konnte. 8. Meine Freunde haben meinen Geburtstag vergessen, worüber ich mich gar nicht freute. 9. Das war das Dümmste, was ich jemals gesehen habe.

7·6 *Sample answers are provided.* 1. Er tanzt mit der Ausländerin, die kein Wort Deutsch versteht. 2. Sie möchte alles wissen, was der Reporter berichtet hat. 3. Der alte Hund ist gestorben, was sehr tragisch ist. 4. Tue nichts, was dich beschämen mag! 5. Die Leute, die den Löwen auf der Straße sahen, fingen an zu schreien. 6. Hamburg ist eine Handelsstadt, deren Hafen weltberühmt ist. 7. Wer lügt, mit dem will ich nichts zu tun haben.

7·7 *Sample answers are provided.* 1. Sie kaufte etwas, was ihr gar nicht gefiel. 2. Kennst du die Mädchen, mit denen Erik spricht? 3. Das Kind, dessen Vater Lehrer ist, ist sehr dumm. 4. Es gibt vieles, worüber ich mich freuen kann.

8 Extended modifiers

8·1 1. ankommend, *arriving* 2. zwingend, *forcing* 3. belastend, *burdening* 4. abstoßend, *pushing away* 5. verhaltend, *restraining* 6. ansehend, *looking at* 7. mitfühlend, *being sympathetic*

8·2 1. die schlafenden Kinder 2. die laut bellenden Hunde 3. von ihrer enttäuschenden Antwort 4. eine entsprechende Theorie 5. neben dem lachenden Jungen 6. im ankommenden Zug 7. das langsam fließende Wasser

8·3 1. ein gebrochener Mann 2. von dem betrunkenen Mann 3. mit den aufgeregten Jungen 4. wegen des schlecht reparierten Motors 5. ein (hart) gekochtes Ei 6. im neulich angekommenen Zug 7. die Vereinigten Staaten

8·4 1. Der den Rechtsanwalt anrufende Polizist ist in Not. 2. Ich hasse das sich so schnell verändernde Wetter. 3. Sein uns überraschender Gewinn erfreute seine Frau. 4. Niemand will dem zum vierten Mal verhafteten Taschendieb helfen. 5. Die langen so trüb brennenden Kerzen standen auf dem Klavier. 6. Das ist der von seinen ehemaligen Studenten besuchte Professor. 7. Sie ist sehr stolz auf die konzentriert arbeitenden Studentinnen.   8. Der an seinen Wunden sterbende Kranke hat keine Familie.   9. Kannten Sie die gestern Abend verstorbene Frau?   10. Der sich so langsam bewegende Soldat war verwundet.

8·5   *Sample answers are provided.*   1. Sie bekam einen von ihrem Freund gut geschriebenen Brief.   2. Er wollte die von seinem Bruder längst aufgegessene Torte probieren.   3. Das vorgestern verkaufte Auto muss schon repariert werden.   4. Gut ausgebildete Menschen werden von unserer Firma gesucht.   5. Die Eltern suchten nach ihrem vor einer Stunde verschwundenen Sohn.   6. Der von seiner zweiten Frau geschiedene Mann will eine jüngere Frau heiraten.   7. Das mit dem Hund spielende Kind fing an zu weinen.

8·6   1. die auf dem Herd stehende Suppe   2. das von der Armee zerstörte Dorf   3. das vor Angst zitternde Kätzchen   4. der laut redende Prediger   5. die vor zwei Jahren gebauten Häuser   6. das brennende und neulich verkaufte Haus   7. die aus zehn Amerikanern bestehende Reisegruppe

8·7   *Sample answers are provided.*   1. Das von dem Studenten getrunkene Bier war gar nicht kalt.   2. Ich kann die von der Köchin gebackene Torte riechen.   3. Das sich die Haare kämmende Mädchen ist meine Freundin.   4. Sie betrachtet die auf dem Boden eingeschlafenen Kinder.

9   Adjectives

9·1   *Sample answers are provided.*   1. a. verstorbenen b. Er wollte von seiner verstorbenen Mutter sprechen.   2. a. großes b. Haben sie ein großes Gebäude gebaut?   3. a. langen b. Der Zug fuhr durch einen langen Tunnel.   4. a. neunen b. Die Studenten jenes neuen Professors haben das Examen bestanden.   5. a. deutschen b. Wir haben Geschenke für unsere deutschen Verwandten.   6. a. ausländishen b. Alle ausländischen Reisenden brauchen ein Visum.   7. a. unartigen b. Er wollte mit beiden unartigen Jungen sprechen.   8. a. scheußlichen b. Sie gingen trotz des scheußlichen Wetters schwimmen.   9. a. langen b. Er ist während einer langen Oper eingeschlafen.   10. a. vorigen b. Sie sollen nicht gegen Ihren vorigen Chef sprechen.

9·2   *Sample answers are provided.*   1. alte, heißen   2. Neue, neuen   3. Unehrlichen   4. kaltes   5. kleiner, hartes   6. schöne, letzten   7. Rote, weiße

9·3   *Sample answers are provided.*   1. manch fleißiger Schüler   2. welch komischer Zufall   3. etwas warme Milch   4. mehr glückliche Tage   5. wenig interessante Bücher   6. von manch fleißigem Schüler   7. zu einem solchen Haus   8. von welch komischen Zufall   9. mit etwas warmer Milch   10. an mehr glücklichen Tagen

9·4   *Sample answers are provided.*   1. vier alte Autos   2. einige komische Witze   3. alle deutschen Touristen   4. mehrere lange Reisen   5. beide weinenden Kinder   6. vier alter Autos   7. einiger komischer Witze   8. aller deutschen Touristen   9. mehrerer langer Reisen   10. beider weinenden Kinder

9·5   1. a. Der braune Hund ist klein. b. Der schwarze Hund ist kleiner als der braune Hund. c. Die weiße Katze ist am kleinsten.   2. a. Sein neuer Roman ist gut. b. Sein letzter Roman ist besser als sein neuer Roman. c. Seine Gedichte sind am besten.   3. a. Diese weiße Kerze ist hell. b. Jene Laterne ist heller als diese weiße Kerze. c. Die neue Stehlampe ist am hellsten.

9·6   *Sample answers are provided.*   1. Bei solch schönem Wetter geht das junge Ehepaar oft spazieren.   2. Eine junge Dame will einen warmen Mantel kaufen.   3. Der Alte erinnerte sich an die frohen Tage seiner Jugend.   4. Diese Schmetterlinge lieben die farbigen, duftenden Rosen.

10   Adverbs

10·1   1. a. Meine Schwester spielt ziemlich gut Geige. b. Meine Schwester spielt recht gut Geige.   2. a. Bach war schon als Kind außerordentlich musikalisch. b. Bach war schon als Kind sehr musikalisch. *Sample adverbs are provided.*   3. a. Meine Tante ist beinahe vierzig Jahre alt. b. Meine Tante ist nur vierzig Jahre alt.   4. a. Der faule Student ist wieder durchgefallen. b. Der faule Student ist leider durchgefallen.

10·2   *Sample answers are provided.*   1. Ihr jüngster Sohn ist wirklich faul.   2. Es gibt heute bestimmt noch Regen.   3. Das kleine Hündchen war sehr schwach und ist leider gestorben.   4. Karl wird uns wahrscheinlich zum Bahnhof begleiten.

10·3   *Sample answers are provided.*   1. Das ist mir ganz egal.   2. Ich kann den alten Mann nicht immer verstehen.   3. Vielleicht hat jemand diesen Regenschirm vergessen.   4. Ich bin niemals in Europa gewesen aber möchte gern dorthin reisen.   5. Die alte Frau geht täglich ins Kino.   6. Plötzlich sah er seinen größten Feind um die Ecke kommen.   7. Ihr müsst das lange Gedicht auswendig lernen.   8. Bist du endlich damit fertig?   9. Warum lügst du immer?   10. Vielleicht kann ich Ihnen damit helfen.

10·4   1. a. Der jüngere Bariton singt schöner. b. Der jüngere Bariton singt am schönsten.   2. a. Diese Jungen haben sich schlechter benommen. b. Diese Jungen haben sich am schlechtesten benommen.   3. a. Mein Onkel wohnt weiter von hier. b. Mein Onkel wohnt am weitesten von hier.   4. a. Sein Vortrag dauerte länger. b. Sein Vortrag dauerte am längsten.

10·5   *Sample answers are provided.*   1. Tina ist wahrscheinlich noch in der Stadt.   2. Musst du immer rauchen?   3. Nächsten Freitag kommen unsere Verwandten zu Besuch.   4. Erik kommt oft spät zur Schule.   5. Wohin reist ihr im Herbst?   6. Vor der Tür stand ein fremder Mann.   7. Diese Geschichte ist ziemlich dumm.

11 Pronouns

11·1   1. Man erwartet von den Bürgern respektiert zu werden.   2. Oft tut man, was man nicht tun soll.   3. Die Firma soll einem mehr Lohn geben.   4. Einem soll so viel wie möglich geholfen werden.   5. Man sagt oft, dass sie miteinander nie auskommen werden.   6. Man muss ihn lange kennen, bis man ihn versteht.   7. Man stand am Fenster und klopfte.

11·2   1. a. Sie hat niemand(em) von dieser Sache erzählt. b. Sie hat jemand(em) von dieser Sache erzählt.   2. a. Ich kannte niemand(en) auf der Geburtstagsfeier. b. Ich kannte jemand(en) auf der Geburtstagsfeier.   3. a. Niemand wollte das alte Haus kaufen. b. Jemand wollte das alte Haus kaufen.   4. a. Du musst doch niemand(em) glauben. b. Du musst doch jemand(em) glauben.

11·3   *Sample answers are provided.*   1. Die Äpfel schmecken sehr gut. Willst du einen?   2. Haben Sie jetzt ein neues Auto? Nein, wir haben keines.   3. Kennst du alle vier Schwestern? Ich kenne nur eine.   4. Spracht ihr mit den sechs Tänzerinnen? Nein, wir sprachen mit einer.

11·4   1. Der Mann und die Frau küssen einander.   2. Martin und Heinz wollen einander besuchen.   3. Frau Keller und Herr Benz fragten nacheinander.   4. Der Franzose und der Schaffner wollten miteinander sprechen.

11·5   *Sample answers are provided.*   1. Sie helfen einander, so viel wie sie können.   2. Sie haben oft voneinander gesprochen.   3. Er stellt die Vasen nebeneinander.   4. Der Mann und seine neue Frau denken oft aneinander.

11·6   1. a. Sie kauft sich neue Schuhe. b. Wir kaufen uns neue Schuhe.   2. a. Sie können sich nicht helfen. b. Ihr könnt euch nicht helfen.   3. a. Er hat sich gewaschen. b. Wer hat sich gewaschen?   4. a. Das wird er sich nie verzeihen. b. Das werde ich mir nie verzeihen.

11·7   *Sample answers are provided.*   1. Hast du dir einen neuen Schlips gefunden?   2. Sie freut sich sehr über das Geschenk.   3. Es bewegt sich nicht.   4. Wir haben uns noch nicht vorgestellt.

12 Infinitives

12·1   *Sample modal auxiliaries are provided.*   1. Sein Vater kann kein Bier trinken.   2. Die kranke Frau musste sich aufs Sofa legen.   3. Ich werde mich rasieren müssen.   4. Der Kellner hat mir die Speisekarte und ein Glas Wasser bringen sollen.   5. Sie durfte mit ihrem neuen Freund ins Theater gehen.   6. Nach dem Essen haben wir in die Stadt fahren müssen.   7. Er will am Wochenende mit seiner Freundin eine Fahrt nach Ulm machen.

12·2   1. Frau Benz hat das zerbrochene Fenster reparieren lassen.   2. Wir werden ein neues Haus im Vorort bauen lassen.   3. Ich ließ einen alten Freund grüßen.   4. Die Mädchen ließen es aus Holz machen.

12·3   *Sample answers are provided.*   1. Das Problem ließ sich kaum lösen.   2. Diese zwei Fenster lassen sich nicht leicht öffnen.   3. Kannst du mir sagen, wo du deine Röcke machen lässt?   4. Martin sagt, dass seine Freundin einen Wagen hat kaufen wollen.

12·4   *Sample answers are provided.*   1. Unsere Nachbarn helfen uns malen.   2. Sehen Sie den Gärtner im Garten arbeiten?   3. Die Kinder hören die Mutter leise schnarchen.   4. Mit der Zeit lernte das Kind gut singen.   5. Niemand lehrte sie Fraktur schreiben.   6. Der alte Hund hörte laute Schritte kommen.   7. Wer lehrt euch weben?

12·5   *Sample answers are provided.*   1. Der Lehrer schickt die Schüler Fußball spielen.   2. Kommt ihr morgen Rad fahren?   3. Jeden Freitag fuhren wir in die Stadt einkaufen.   4. Die Touristen kamen mit uns bummeln.

12·6 *Sample answers are provided.* 1. Seine Eltern mussten den bösen Hund wegjagen. 2. Unser Onkel mag gern guten Wein trinken. 3. Hast du ihn ins Schlafzimmer kommen hören? 4. Meine Tante schickte mich oft zum Einkaufszentrum einkaufen.

12·7 *Sample answers are provided.* 1. Hast du den schönen Kinderchor singen hören? 2. Frau Müller muss bald ins Ausland reisen. 3. Warum schickst du mich immer einkaufen? 4. Wir sahen die beste Mannschaft spielen. 5. Der faule Junge lernt nicht lesen. 6. Kommt ihr morgen Schlittschuh laufen? 7. Er hat sich den neuen Anzug reinigen lassen.

13 Short responses

13·1 *Sample answers are provided.* 1. Wie schnell kann das Pferd laufen? 2. Erik kennt sie gar nicht, aber er sieht sie jeden Tag an der Ecke stehen. 3. Kaum zu glauben! 4. Der hochnäsige Student ist gar nicht so intelligent. 5. Der Dieb ist doch auch ein Lügner! 6. Also, bis morgen. Schlaf gut! 7. „Du hast deine Handschuhe wieder verloren!" „Doch nicht!"

13·2 *Sample answers are provided.* 1. Also, gehen wir schon! 2. Das ist doch nicht wahr! 3. Ich verstehe gar nicht, warum du lügst. 4. Sei mal ruhig! 5. Seine Worte sind kaum zu verstehen. 6. Wie kommt so etwas? 7. Ich komme morgen zu euch, und zwar um elf Uhr.

13·3 *Sample sentences are provided.* 1. Ausgezeichnet! 2. Erstaunlich! 3. Offenbar. 4. Keine Ahnung. 5. Großartig! 6. Leider nicht. 7. Selbstverständlich.

13·4 *Sample answers are provided.* 1. Kannst du mir fünfzig Euro leihen? 2. Alle zwei Minuten startet ein Flugzeug von diesem Flughafen. 3. Ist Andrea achtzehn oder neunzehn Jahre alt? 4. Unsere Mannschaft hat den Pokal gewonnen. 5. Sie ist eine sehr gute Tänzerin. 6. Nach zwei Jahren haben sie das Problem endlich gelöst. 7. Ich möchte dir ein paar neue CDs kaufen.

14 Idioms and special phrases

14·1 *Sample answers are provided.* 1. Tina hat den neuen Studenten gern. 2. Hast du Frau Schneider gern? 3. Alle haben dich gern. 4. Ich habe diese betrunkenen Männer gar nicht gern. 5. Wir wandern gern im Wald. 6. Ich reise nicht gern im Winter. 7. Sie ruht sich gern auf der Terrasse aus.

14·2 1. a. Ich habe diese Frau nicht gern. b. Ich habe solche Leute nicht gern. 2. a. Das hättet ihr nicht fragen sollen. b. Das hätten Sie nicht fragen sollen. 3. a. Sein Vater wird vor die Hunde gehen. b. Diese Pläne werden vor die Hunde gehen. 4. a. Ich freue mich schon auf deinen Aufenthalt in Bremen. b. Ich freue mich schon auf euren Besuch. 5. a. Hast du Lust Freunde in der Stadt zu besuchen? b. Hast du Lust fernzusehen? 6. a. Ich habe diese dummen Witze wirklich satt! b. Ich habe deine andauernden Fragen wirklich satt!

14·3 *Sample answers are provided.* 1. Ist Hcrr Bauer ein Freund von dir? 2. Meine Schwester ist endlich zur Party gekommen. 3. Warum hinkt der Mann so? 4. Deine Freundin tanzt wieder mit dem blonden Typ! 5. Arbeitet Frau Schneider noch bei der Bank? 6. Sehe ich wirklich wie eine Prinzessin aus? 7. Ich bin intelligenter als die anderen. Bescheidener auch!

14·4 *Sample answers are provided.* 1. Wie immer schwatzt er. 2. Ja, die Frau ist wieder in andern Umständen. 3. Prima! 4. Er ist diese Woche nicht bei Kasse.

14·5 *Sample answers are provided.* 1. a. Beeilt euch! b. Beeilen Sie sich! 2. a. Die Firma will sich von Herrn Keller trennen. b. Die Firma will sich von der neuen Managerin trennen. 3. a. Deine Frau fürchtet sich vor dir. b. Ich fürchte mich vor dir. 4. a. Er hat sich mit Tapferkeit benommen. b. Er hat sich artig benommen. 5. a. Erinnern Sie sich daran? b. Erinnert ihr euch daran? 6. a. Ich kann mich nicht an das laute Bellen gewöhnen. b. Ich kann mich nicht an ihre Stimme gewöhnen. 7. a. Ich habe mich zur Heirat entschlossen. b. Tina hat sich zur Heirat entschlossen.

15 Antonyms and contrasts

15·1 *Sample answers are provided.* 1. Nein. Ich habe kein Wasser. Ich verdurste. 2. Nein, sie sind gestern nacht schon abgefahren. 3. Leider nicht. Sie wird von mir nur eine Geburtstagskarte bekommen. 4. Nein. Er hat es mir verboten mein Geld zu verschwenden. 5. O, nein. Sie ist sehr froh und lacht wieder. 6. Nein, die armen Menschen verhungern. 7. Welch eine Idee! Unser Haus wollen wir nicht verkaufen!

8. Nicht heute. Ich gehe nach Hause.   9. Nein. Ich liebe alle Arten Musik.   10. Überhaupt nicht. Sein Bruder hat ihn mir geschickt.

15·2   *Sample answers are provided.*   1. Ist eine Ebene immer leichter zu erobern als ein Berg?   2. Ist die Freude nicht sanfter als der Zorn?   3. Würdest du lieber in Gefangenschaft leben als in Freiheit?   4. Ist Gott nicht mächtiger als der Teufel?   5. Kann ein Herr vornehmer als eine Dame sein?   6. Würdest du lieber in der Hölle leben als im Himmel?   7. Kann ein Junge wirklich besser spielen als ein Mädchen?   8. Kannst du die Hitze leichter ertragen als die Kälte?   9. Ist ein Kind nicht mehr zu schätzen als ein Erwachsener?   10. Findest du Komödie nicht interessanter als Tragödie?   11. Ist Krankheit nicht fürchterlicher als Gesundheit?   12. Ist so ein Krieg wirklich wichtiger als der Frieden?   13. Ist das Leben nicht süßer als der Tod?   14. Kann der Lehrling schneller arbeiten als sein Meister?   15. Ist Liebe nicht stärker als Hass?   16. Ist ein Mann immer weniger emotionell als eine Frau?   17. Ist Reichtum wirklich besser als Armut?   18. Muss die Spitze kleiner als die Sohle sein?   19. Hast du größere Angst am Tag oder in der Nacht?   20. Ist die Vorderseite schmutziger als die Rückseite?

15·3   *Sample answers are provided.*   1. Der Riese ist nicht schwach, sondern unheimlich stark.   2. Der Schreibtisch ist nicht wackelig, sondern stabil.   3. Unser Schlafzimmer ist nicht hell, sondern dunkel.   4. Der Pilot ist nicht unerfahren, sondern sehr erfahren.   5. Die Straßen sind noch nicht trocken, sondern noch sehr nass.   6. Der Boden muss nicht schmutzig sein, sondern sauber.   7. Die Gäste sind noch nicht satt, sondern sehr hungrig.   8. Das Glas ist nicht glänzend, sondern matt.   9. Der Mörder war nicht warmblütig, sondern kaltblütig.   10. Diese Kinder sind nicht fleißig, sondern faul.

15·4   *Sample answers are provided.*   1. Ist der neue Student wirklich klüger als Professor Keller?   2. Dieser Witz ist viel komischer als die anderen.   3. Seine Freundin ist eingebildeter als er.   4. Die Alpen sind höher als der Harz.   5. Martin war ein bisschen lerneifriger als sein Cousin.   6. Der Tisch ist viel wackliger als die Stühle.   7. Heute ist der Himmel dunkler als gestern.   8. Der neue König ist schrecklicher als sein Vater.   9. Der amerikanische Wagen ist ein bisschen preiswerter als der deutsche.   10. Meine Tochter benimmt sich viel artiger als mein Sohn.

15·5   *Sample answers are provided.*   1. a. Tulpen riechen schlechter als Nelken. b. Rosen duften am besten.   2. a. Ein Igel ist kleiner als eine Katze. b. Ein Löwe ist am größten.   3. a. Der Milchladen ist niedriger als das Rathaus. b. Der Dom ist am höchsten.   4. a. Der Schüler ist viel dümmer als die Lehrerin. b. Am klügsten ist der Professor.   5. a. Auf einer tropischen Insel ist es wärmer als in Italien. b. In Sibirien ist es am kältesten.   6. a. Der Economywagen ist ein bisschen leichter als der VW. b. Der Mercedes Benz ist am schwersten.   7. a. Ein Wurm ist viel kürzer als eine Klapperschlange. b. Eine Anakonda ist aber am längsten.   8. a. Essig ist saurer als Sauerrahm. b. Ein Pflaumenkuchen ist am süßesten.   9. a. Eine Schlange ist dünner als ein Wolf. b. Ein Bär ist am dicksten.   10. a. Ein Luftschiff fliegt viel langsamer als ein Doppeldecker. b. Am schnellsten fliegt ein Düsenjäger.

16   The passive voice

16·1   1. a. Die Briefe wurden von mir geschickt. b. Die Briefe sind von mir geschickt worden. c. Die Briefe werden von mir geschickt werden.   2. a. Die Aufgaben werden von den Schülern gemacht. b. Die Aufgaben sind von den Schülern gemacht worden. c. Die Aufgaben werden von den Schülern gemacht werden.   3. a. Der Ball wurde von den Kindern gesucht. b. Der Ball ist von den Kindern gesucht worden. c. Der Ball wird von den Kindern gesucht werden.   4. a. Eine neue Stadt wird von den Entdeckungsreisenden gegründet. b. Eine neue Stadt wurde von den Entdeckungsreisenden gegründet. c. Eine neue Stadt wird von den Entdeckungsreisenden gegründet werden.   5. a. Das Haus wird von den Arbeitern gebaut. b. Das Haus wurde von den Arbeitern gebaut. c. Das Haus ist von den Arbeitern gebaut worden.   6. a. Dieses Fest wurde von vielen Menschen gefeiert. b. Dieses Fest ist von vielen Menschen gefeiert worden. c. Dieses Fest wird von vielen Menschen gefeiert werden.   7. a. Im 21. Jahrhundert werden die ersten elektrischen Autos von ihnen gebaut. b. Im 21. Jahrhundert sind die ersten elektrischen Autos von ihnen gebaut worden. c. Im 21. Jahrhundert werden die ersten elektrischen Autos von ihnen gebaut werden.

16·2   1. Das Wort ist von der Lehrerin buchstabiert worden.   2. Das riesige Düsenflugzeug wurde von Herrn Schneider fotografiert.   3. Das kleine Dorf ist durch Bomben zerstört worden.   4. Ein Mittel gegen Heuschnupfen wird von dem Arzt verschrieben werden.   5. Oft wird das eigene Leben von mutigen Männern für die Wissenschaft geopfert.   6. Drei Einzelzimmer wurden von der Wirtin vermietet.   7. Im 15. Jahrhundert ist die Bibel von Gutenberg gedruckt worden.   8. Zwei Gläser Bier werden von der Kellnerin gebracht.   9. Ihr Geburtstag ist wieder vergessen worden.   10. Seine Eltern wurden von dem faulen Sohn enttäuscht.   11. Alle Krankheiten werden niemals von den Wissenschaftlern geheilt werden.

12. Der Diplomat wird von der Professorin vorgestellt.   13. Der Vortrag ist von Frau Doktor Keller gehalten worden.   14. Viele Ansichtskarten werden von den Ausländern gebraucht.

16·3   1. a. Jedem Schüler wurde ein Bleistift von der Lehrerin gegeben.   b. Jedem Schüler ist ein Bleistift von der Lehrerin gegeben worden.   c. Jedem Schüler wird ein Bleistift von der Lehrerin gegeben werden.   2. a. Seinen Eltern wird ein CD-Player geschenkt.   b. Seinen Eltern wurde ein CD-Player geschenkt.   c. Seinen Eltern ist ein CD-Player geschenkt worden.   3. a. Ihnen werden die Bilder vom Reiseführer gezeigt.   b. Ihnen sind die Bilder vom Reiseführer gezeigt worden.   c. Ihnen werden die Bilder vom Reiseführer gezeigt werden.

16·4   *Word order may vary.*   1. Dem Kranken wurde ein Kissen gebracht.   2. Ihnen werden Ansichtskarten von den Reisenden gesandt.   3. Die Waren sind Herrn Braun von der Firma ins Haus gesandt worden.   4. Wem werden diese Geschenke von den Mädchen gegeben?   5. Dem neuen Studenten sind die Videos von meiner Schwester geliehen worden.   6. Was ist der Kanzlerin von dem Diplomaten versprochen worden?   7. Was wird den Gastgebern von dir gebracht?   8. Dem neuen Dozenten ist ein teurer Füller von der Professorin geschenkt worden.   9. Dem Stürmer wurde der Ball von dem Torwart geworfen.

16·5   1. a. Dem Professor wurde von ihren Gedichten sehr imponiert.   b. Dem Professor ist von ihren Gedichten sehr imponiert worden.   c. Dem Professor wird von ihren Gedichten sehr imponiert werden.   2. a. Dem Lehrer wird nicht geantwortet.   b. Dem Lehrer ist nicht geantwortet worden.   c. Dem Lehrer wird nicht geantwortet werden.   3. a. Der Wirtin wird mit einer Geldstrafe gedroht.   b. Der Wirtin wurde mit einer Geldstrafe gedroht.   c. Der Wirtin ist mit einer Geldstrafe gedroht worden.

16·6   1. Einem Germanisten wird von einem guten Wörterbuch genützt werden.   2. Solchen Politikern wird nie vertraut werden.   3. Ihm ist kaum zugehört worden.   4. Ist dem Meister von den frechen Lehrlingen widersprochen worden?   5. Der Gerechtigkeit wird davon nicht gedient werden.   6. Ihr wurde andauernd von dem Trickbetrüger geschmeichelt.   7. Warum wird mir nicht geglaubt?

16·7   *Sample answers are provided.*   1. a. Der Manager wird von dem Chef entlassen werden.   b. Der Manager wird von der Generaldirektorin entlassen werden.   c. Der Manager wird von der Firma entlassen werden.   2. a. Die alten Häuser sind durch einen starken Wind zerstört worden.   b. Die alten Häuser sind durch ein Erdbeben zerstört worden.   c. Die alten Häuser sind durch eine Überschwemmung zerstört worden.

16·8   1. a. Der Säugling muss von der Mutter gefüttert werden.   b. Der Säugling hat von der Mutter gefüttert werden müssen.   2. a. Die Gäste wollen nicht schnell bedient werden.   b. Die Gäste haben nicht schnell bedient werden wollen.   3. a. Der Artikel soll von dem besten Reporter geschrieben werden.   b. Der Artikel hat von dem besten Reporter geschrieben werden sollen.   4. a. Das Brot kann nicht in einer halben Stunde gebacken werden.   b. Das Brot hat nicht in einer halben Stunde gebacken werden können.

16·9   *Sample answers are provided.*   1. Erik muss sofort vom Bahnhof abgeholt werden.   2. Diese Klasse sollte von einem anderen Lehrer unterrichtet werden.   3. Der Aufsatz kann nicht schneller geschrieben werden.   4. Solche Wörter dürfen nicht geschrieben werden.   5. Eine saubere Wohnung muss bald gemietet werden.   6. Ihre alte Tante soll oft besucht werden.   7. Der Chef darf nicht in diesem Ton angesprochen werden.

16·10   1. Der verwundete Mann war gerettet.   2. Die Haustiere sind gefüttert.   3. Die unartigen Kinder sind bestraft.   4. Die schöne Tasse war leider zerbrochen. *Sample answers are provided.*   5. Die arme Frau wurde verletzt. Die arme Frau war verletzt.   6. Die Fenster wurden geöffnet. Die Fenster sind geöffnet.   7. Meine Brieftasche wird verloren. Meine Brieftasche ist verloren.

17   The subjunctive mood

17·1   1. helfe, hälfe   2. bleibe, bliebe   3. besuche, besuchte   4. bringe mit, brächte mit   5. sei gekommen, wäre gekommen   6. werde sprechen, würde sprechen   7. müsse lachen, müsste lachen   8. esse, äße   9. nenne, nennte   10. werde gefunden werden, würde gefunden werden

17·2   *Sample answers are provided.*   1. a. Der Reporter berichtete, dass die junge Schauspielerin ihn geküsst habe.   b. dass jemand seine Brieftasche gestohlen habe.   c. dass der alte König nicht mehr regieren könne.   d. dass die Kanzlerin in Berlin bleiben werde.   2. a. Professor Benz fragte, ob der Student einen Aufsatz schreibe.   b. ob sein Kollege eine neue Stellung gefunden habe.   c. ob sein Sohn sich gut benehme.   d. ob das Feuer die Bibliothek zerstört habe.   3. a. Sie teilte mit, dass der Dieb bestraft werde.   b. dass die Armee das kleine Dorf verteidigen müsse.   c. dass die Gemeinde eine neue Kirche nicht bauen könne.   d. dass die Zeugen nichts gesehen hätten.   4. a. Frau Kamps erzählte, dass seine Geschichte ihr kaum imponiere.   b. dass der Millionär sehr wenig Geld ausgeben wolle.   c. dass sie seine Fehler verbessert habe.   d. dass der Feind nicht angreifen könne.

17·3   *Sample answers are provided.*   1. a. Meine Schwester tut so, als ob sie sehr intelligent wäre. b. als ob das Wetter schön wäre. c. als ob sie helfen wollte.   2. a. Der alte Mann lacht, als ob er nicht krank wäre. b. als ob seine Frau nicht gestorben wäre. c. als ob er den Witz verstünde.   3. a. Die Kinder singen, als ob sie schöne Stimmen hätten. b. als ob sie die Worte wirklich verstünden. c. als ob das Volkslied eine Oper wäre.   4. a. Meine Mutter weinte, als ob ich gestorben wäre. b. als ob wir arm geworden wären. c. als ob es eine Tragödie wäre.

17·4   1. a. Wenn ihr nur bei mir wäret! b. Wäret ihr nur bei mir!   2. a. Wenn das Kind nur fleißig wäre! b. Wäre das Kind nur fleißig!   3. a. Wenn der arme Mann doch nicht so unglücklich wäre! b. Wäre der arme Mann doch nicht so unglücklich!   4. a. Wenn ich ihnen nur helfen könnte! b. Könnte ich ihnen nur helfen!   5. a. Wenn du mehr Glück gehabt hättest! b. Hättest du mehr Glück gehabt!

17·5   *Sample answers are provided.*   1. Wenn der Wagen nicht kaputt wäre, würden wir in die Stadt fahren.   2. Wenn es nicht regnete, könnten die Jungen im Garten spielen.   3. Wenn ich den Zug verpasste, würde ich in Hamburg übernachten.   4. Wenn ihr Kind wieder gesund wäre, würde sie aufhören zu weinen.   5. Wenn Erik reicher wäre, würde er einen Rennwagen kaufen.   6. Wenn Onkel Hans das Klavier spielen könnte, könnten die Mädchen tanzen.   7. Wenn Frau Benz ihn kennte, würde sie ihn einladen.   8. Wenn sie auf dem Balkon stünden, könnten sie das ganze Dorf sehen.

17·6   *Sample answers are provided.*   1. Wenn wir in Süddeutschland gewesen wären, wären wir nach München gefahren.   2. Wenn der Kerl hilfsbereit gewesen wäre, hätte er länger bleiben können.   3. Wenn es das Medikament genommen hätte, wäre das Kind schneller gesund geworden.   4. Wenn sie besser Deutsch hätte sprechen können, hätte ich ihre Rede verstanden.   5. Wenn Sonja nicht krank gewesen wäre, wäre sie zum Faschingsfest gegangen.   6. Wenn das Wetter besser geworden wäre, wären wir noch einen Tag in den Bergen geblieben.   7. Wenn ich einen neuen Laptop gekauft hätte, hätte ich den Aufsatz schneller schreiben können.   8. Wenn das Baby hätte schlafen können, hätte es nicht andauernd geweint.

17·7   *Sample answers are provided.*   1. Wenn Sabine nach Hause käme, würde ihre Mutter sehr glücklich sein.   2. Wenn der Bus pünktlich gekommen wäre, wären wir nicht so böse gewesen.   3. Wenn wir Thomas damit geholfen hätten, wäre er noch unser Freund gewesen.   4. Wenn ich das gewusst hätte, hätte ich nicht danach gefragt.   5. Wenn der Schüler aufmerksam wäre, würde er keine Fehler machen.   6. Wenn sie wieder gesund wäre, würde Vater wieder froh sein.   7. Wenn sie mehr Geld hätte, würde sie immer noch Probleme haben.   8. Wenn Tina in die Stadt gefahren wäre, hätte ich mit den Kindern zu Hause bleiben müssen.   9. Wenn ihr Mann noch zu Hause gewesen wäre, wäre Frau Keller zum Park gegangen.   10. Wenn es nicht so kalt wäre, dann würden wir schwimmen gehen.

17·8   *Sample answers are provided.*   1. Wenn der Polizist nicht so aufmerksam wäre, würde der Taschendieb eine Handtasche stehlen.   2. Wenn ihre Cousine zu Besuch käme, würden Sabine und Renate sich freuen.   3. Wenn die Kellnerin netter wäre, würden die Gäste länger bleiben.   4. Wenn der Sauerbraten schon durchgekocht wäre, würde die Köchin die Kartoffeln kochen.

18   Punctuation

18·1   *Sample answers are provided.*   1. Wann kommt der nächste Zug ?   2. Wenn sie es verstünde, würde sie keine Fragen haben .   3. Ist deine Tante wieder krank geworden ?   4. Haben sie keine Kinder ?   5. Ist die Ostsee rauher als die Nordsee ?   6. Die Kunden gehen in den Laden und kaufen was sie brauchen .   7. Hing ein Schild über der Tür des Ladens ?   8. Wer steht in der Ecke im Wohnzimmer ?   9. Mein Bruder ist am 6 . April geboren.   10. Ist der Inter-City schneller als der Eilzug ?

18·2   *Sample answers are provided.*   1. Thomas vergisst, dass der Aufsatz heute fällig ist.   2. Seine Frau interessiert sich nicht für Wildwestfilme.   3. Martin freut sich schon aufs Wochenende.   4. Sind die Wellen heute größer als gestern?   5. Ist Sonja so schön wie ihre Schwester?   6. Muss ich wieder um fünf Uhr aufstehen?   7. Werden sie sich endlich darüber unterhalten?   8. Wann ist das kleine Schiff untergegangen?   9. Was für ein Tier trifft das Rotkäppchen im Wald?   10. Warum hat die Ente den Kopf ins Wasser getaucht?

18·3   1. In der alten Eisenbahn X saßen sie auf Bänken , oder standen in den Gängen.   2. Er wird zwischen dem vierten X und dem sechsten Juni abreisen.   3. Frau Keller , die Vorsitzende der Firma , war gar nicht zufrieden.   4. Die alte Dame , rot vor Erregung , konnte nicht sprechen.   5. Ich habe einen alten Schulkameraden angerufen , als ich in Oldenburg war.   6. Er lief an die Tür , um sie aufzumachen.   7. Der Professor , der sehr populär war , fragte , ob seine Studenten auf das Examen vorbereitet seien.

18·4   *Sample answers are provided.*   1. Professor Benz, der mehr als vierzig Jahre an der Uni war, war sehr enttäuscht.   2. Als wir in Garmisch-Partenkirchen ankamen, fing es an zu schneien.   3. Der Junge probierte den Kuchen, ohne seine Mutter zu fragen. 4. Sie brachte ihre beiden Brüder, ihre Schwester und ihre Cousine mit. 5. Der Offizier ordnete an das Dorf anzugreifen. 6. Seine Verlobte, außer sich vor Freude, fing an zu lachen. 7. Meine Verwandten sind gekommen, um Weihnachten mit uns zu feiern

18·5 *Sample answers are provided.* 1. Er wollte kein Gemüse essen, denn er isst lieber Obst. 2. Wie lange müssen wir warten, bis der Zug abfährt? 3. Es hat nicht geregnet, sondern geschneit. 4. Reist ihr lieber mit dem Fahrrad, dem Zug oder dem Flugzeug? 5. Das Kind reitet auf einem Esel, weil das Pferd zu groß ist. 6. Liest Tina die Zeitung, oder schreibt sie einen Brief? 7. Ich glaube, dass die Zukunft viel besser wird.

18·6 1. Die Richterin sagte zu dem Angeklagten : „Sie müssen antworten , wenn ich Sie frage ." 2. Seien Sie vernunftig ! 3. Vorsicht ! Zutritt verboten ! 4. Die Klägerin behauptete : „Der Hausmakler hat mich betrogen ." 5. Die bestehenden Gesetze müssen beachtet werden ; *or* , vor allem müssen die Richter und Anwälte jedes Gesetz genau befolgen. 6. Die Krankenschwestern müssen , solange Ärzte da sind , nicht selbstständig , sondern nach deren Anweisung handeln . 7. Reisen jetzt viele Menschen im Flugzeug , weil es schneller ist , oder weil es nicht mehr gefährlich ist ?

19 Letter writing

19·1 1. a. Frau b. Dorothea Schäfer c. Hauptstr. 11 d. 67021 Ludwigshafen 2. a. Firma b. Klassen & Meyer c. z. H. Herrn Hermann Fitz d. Hochstr. 55 e. 17712 Berlin

19·2 *Sample salutations and closings are provided.* 1. a. Berlin, 6. 6. 2008 b. Sehr geehrter Herr Doktor c. Mit freundlichen Grüßen 2. a. Bremen, d. 29.3.2009 b. Liebe Sonja! c. Alles Liebe

19·3 *A sample letter is provided.*

Bremen, d. 2. 5. 2008

Liebe Tina!

Ich möchte dich ganz herzlich für das schöne, gestreifte Hemd danken, das du mir zu meinem Geburtstag geschenkt hast. Es passt mir gut und sieht mit meinem braunen Sakko gut aus.

Es war auch gut zu hören, dass es deiner Mutter wieder gut geht. Ich freue mich schon darauf, dass ihr beide mich bald besuchen werdet.

Alles Liebe

dein Boris

19·4 *A sample letter is provided.*

Bonn, d. 11. 9. 2008

Hotel Neumann

Domstr. 80

86011 München

Zimmerreservierung

Sehr geehrte Damen und Herren,

ich habe Ihre Anschrift der Broschüre „Hotels in Bayern" entnommen und möchte für die Woche von Dienstag, 10. 2. bis Montag, 17. 2. ein zum Garten gelegenes Doppelzimmer reservieren. Ich würde mit meiner Tochter kommen. Falls Sie etwas Passendes frei haben, teilen Sie mir doch bitte den Preis mit.

Ich freue mich darauf, bald von Ihnen zu hören und verbleibe

Mit freundlichen Grüßen

Ihre

Ingrid Kamps

19·5 *A sample e-mail message is provided.*

Liebe Sabine,

meine Schwester Angela hat am Montag Geburtstag, und ich habe noch kein Geburtstagsgeschenk. Was Angela nur möchte? Eine Bluse? Einen Pullover? Oder vielleicht eine CD? Aber CDs kosten so viel, und ich habe nur fünfzehn Euro für ein Geschenk. Vielleicht ein Buch. Aber Paperbacks sind zu billig! Kannst du mir helfen?

Erik

20 Let's write!

20·1 *Sample answers are provided.* 1. Seine Freundin hat sich über den Blumenstrauß gefreut, den er ihr zum Geburtstag geschickt hat. 2. Der neue Zollbeamte wurde entlassen, weil er oft betrunken war und spät zur Arbeit kam. 3. Als Frau Keller in der Hauptstadt war, hat sie viele Abgeordnete des Bundestags interviewt und fotografiert. 4. Wir würden im Winter öfter nach Schweden reisen, wenn ich das kalte Wetter ertragen könnte. 5. Hoffentlich wird meine ehemalige Freundin meine neue Freundin nicht auf der Hochzeitsfeier treffen. 6. Vor einer Woche wurde die alte Scheune durch eine Bombe zerstört. 7. Er hat sich benommen, als ob er den ersten Preis gewonnen hätte.

20·2 *Sample answers are provided.* 1. Der Reporter berichtete, dass der Friedensvertrag noch nicht unterzeichnet worden sei. 2. Ich will am Wochenende eine Fahrt mit meiner Freundin nach Koblenz machen. 3. Am Schalter lösen wir die Fahrkarten und fangen an auf den Bus zu warten. 4. Sie steckte das Geld in ihre Tasche, weil sie Angst hatte, dass sie es verlieren wird. 5. Tina schreibt Briefe an ihre Familie in der Heimat und muss dann noch etwas arbeiten. 6. Um wie viel Uhr fängt das Rockkonzert an? 7. Wenn ich ihn besser kennen würde, würde ich ihn zum Faschingsfest einladen. 8. Wie viel Grad sind es mitten im Sommer im Schatten? 9. Martin ist um sechs aufgestanden, um die Enten zu füttern. 10. Die Kühe und Schweine wurden jeden Morgen von der Bäuerin gefüttert. 11. Ein schreckliches Gewitter ergriff die Stadt, als wir Onkel Peter in Bonn besuchten. 12. In einem weit entfernten Land gründeten sie eine neue Stadt. 13. Der Professor wird einen Vortrag halten und ein Video darüber zeigen. 14. Die beiden Brüder streiten sich immer wie Hund und Katze.

20·3 *Sample answers are provided.* 1. fleißigen, Der Vater der fleißigen Schülerin ist sehr zufrieden. 2. amerikanischen, mittelalterliche, Die amerikanischen Reisenden haben viele mittelalterliche Kirchen besichtigt. 3. reiche, gebrauchten, Warum hat dieser reiche Herr seinen gebrauchten Sportwagen verkaufen wollen? 4. nächstes, schattigen, Wird Ihr nächstes Mietshaus auch in dieser schattigen Gasse gebaut werden? 5. einsame, unehrlichen, Warum wird der einsame Student diesem unehrlichen Kerl Geld borgen? 6. ältester, unschuldig, Die junge Dame sagte, dass ihr ältester Bruder ganz unschuldig sei. 7. winzigen, gute, lange, Der Bürgermeister des winzigen Dorfes freute sich sehr auf die gute Nachricht, dass der lange Sturm endlich vorbei ist. 8. wollene, baumwollenes, warme, Sie kaufte keine wollenen Straßenkleider, sondern nur eine baumwollene Schürze und zwei warme Halstücher. 9. tragenden, jeden, köstlichsten, Die reichlich tragenden Kirschbäume beschenken uns jeden Sommer mit den köstlichsten Kirschen. 10. schönen, kleine, große, schattiger, In dem schönen Blumengarten gibt es einen kleinen See und eine große Zahl schattiger Spazierwege.

20·4 *Sample answers are provided.* 1. Dieses Kopiergerät ist ebenso teuer wie das neue Faxgerät. 2. Die teuersten Rasierklingen waren wirklich viel schärfer als diese billigen. 3. Der junge Frosch wird weiter springen als der alte, dicke Frosch. 4. Sein neuestes Werk war doch am längsten. 5. Er hat eine viel hübschere Orchidee als Thomas gekauft. 6. Welcher ist der kürzeste Weg zum Stadtpark? 7. Die deutsche Marke wird nicht billiger als die japanische sein. 8. Hast du den Artikel vollendet, oder musst du noch daran arbeiten? 9. Der neue Schüler ist gar nicht fleißiger als die anderen. 10. Der Bodensee war wahrscheinlich der tiefste.

20·5 *Sample answers are provided.* 1. a. seine vielen Probleme b. die letzte Wahl c. eine bessere Organisation d. Erdkunde e. das Leben eines Urwaldmenschen 2. a. weil ich es nicht verstehen kann b. weil es zu schmutzig ist c. wegen seines schlechten Benehmens d. weil ich keine Zeit habe e. weil er gut ausgebildet ist 3. a. nach Hause b. bis an die Mauer c. zum Hafen d. hierher um die Ecke e. ins Restaurant 4. a. ein warmes Sweatshirt b. eine Tasse aus Glas c. eine goldene Krone d. eine Lederjacke e. ein Buch mit bunten Bildern 5. a. der rote Schlips b. ihr neues Ballkleid c. sein letzter Roman d. der alte Herr links

e. die hübsche Frau im Garten   6. a. achtzig Kilometer von hier b. bis ans Ende der Straße c. nicht weit von hier d. vier Straßen von hier entfernt e. an der anderen Seite des Parks   7. a. alle paar Tage b. zehnmal im Jahr c. so oft wie möglich d. fünfmal pro Tag e. jeden zweiten Montag

20·6

20·7   *Sample structures for your paragraph are provided.*   a. Der deutsche Tourist teilte mit, dass er gut angekommen sei. b. Wenn der Schüler nicht aufmerksam wäre, würde er viele Fehler machen. c. Der Staat, an dessen Spitze ein Präsident steht, ist eine Republik.

20·8   *Sample structures for your paragraph are provided.*   a. Er sprach über seinen eigenen Bruder, als ob er sein ärgster Feind wäre. b. Die fleißige Schülerin ist von ihrer Lehrerin gelobt worden. c. Ich möchte gern ein Buch über die Philosophie des achtzehnten Jahrhunderts.